FULFILLING THE PROMISE OF EXCELLENCE

A Practitioner's Guide to School Improvement

FULFILLING THE PROMISE OF EXCELLENCE

A Practitioner's Guide to School Improvement

Richard DuFour
and
Robert Eaker

J. L. Wilkerson Publishing Company
P.O. Box 948
Westbury, New York 11590

Library of Congress Cataloging-in-Publication Data

DuFour, Richard, 1947–
  Fulfilling the promise of excellence.

  Bibliography: p.
  Includes index.
  1. School improvement programs—United States.
2. School supervision—United States.   3. School
management and organization—United States.
I. Eaker, Robert E.   II. Title.
LB2822.82.D83   1987   371.2   86-40358
ISBN 0-915253-06-2

© Richard DuFour and Robert E. Eaker 1987

Acknowledgments

We wish to thank Lynda Fox, Tish Moody and Thelma Sloan for their patience and diligence as they labored over the typing of the multiple drafts of the manuscript. We both owe a special debt to Dr. Jerry Bellon who has acted as a mentor and friend throughout most of our professional careers. We recognize and appreciate the special men and women of Adlai Stevenson High School whose professionalism and dedication have helped to create an environment in which the ideas presented in this book could flourish. Finally, our gratitude goes to our wives, Susan DuFour and Star Eaker, for their support and encouragement during the many months that we were preoccupied with the writing of this book.

Dedication

To Jewel Eaker, my mother; Star, my wife; Carrie and Robin, my children; and in memory of Raymond Eaker, my father. R.E.

To Susan and Matthew. R.D.

CONTENTS

Foreword

For several decades, the public schools have been the target of reform and improvement initiatives. Innovation in the 1960's. Accountability and improvement in the 1970's. The themes have changed as have the sponsors. At various times, impetus for change has come from local, state and federal levels of government as well as from within the educational profession itself.

Our 1980's version of the ongoing series has featured a national commission, state commissions and legislation from Alaska to Florida, as well as a variety of events and programs that have been sponsored at the local level. The primary goal: to improve the public schools, a critical objective in a democracy where an educated populace is a prerequisite to success.

But as worthy as educational improvement goals seem, a reform movement is a complicated event. It has several audiences. One is composed of policy-makers, policy-watchers, and citizens at-large. This group has watched intently as recommendations of commissions have been shaped, as legislation has been drafted, and as top officials have articulated their commitment and concern. Another audience includes the citizens and parents of local communities. While interested in the larger reform scene, these spectators focus their attention on the local school board and superintendent and the principals and teachers of the various schools. They want to be reassured that their schools are either excellent or in the process of becoming so. A third audience, relatively uninterested in the drama, is a hard-minded crowd of analysts and academics—critics who want some tangible evidence that schools are better now than before all the activity began. They are waiting in the wings until reviews, box office returns, and other evidence are accumulated and broadcast.

Amidst all of these diverse audiences is a seasoned, tired, and wary group of players—teachers and administrators. Many have been through all this in one form or another, time after time before. Deep down, they know their business. They are acutely aware that much of what the audience wants from them is already being delivered. They also see in reform programs suggestions that are in concert with improvements they already know are needed. Between the lines they sense some elements of the reform that could destroy the drama for most audiences if they were really taken seriously and put into practice.

One of the problems confronting the players—superintendents, principals, and teachers—being asked to improve the school is that they often are unsure of exactly how to proceed. In addition to diverse audiences all wanting something different, there is a cacophony of voices suggesting how it should be done differently. Some experts advocate the adoption of specific characteristics or attributes; others suggest that schools should emulate organizations in for-profit sectors; still others outline specific strategies for improvement.

What can we legitimately expect from the 1980's reform efforts? If history is our guide, the outcome is fairly certain. Very little of any significance in schools will be changed. If we are fortunate, the activity itself will reaffirm our faith and confidence in our educational institutions. In many cases, thoughtful educators will use the reform initiatives as an opportunity to revitalize or refurbish outmoded patterns and practices. But when all the dust settles, a fundamental law will once again be reaffirmed. Human organizations are built, rebuilt, and remodeled from within. Raw materials and motivation can be imported from outside, but the actual work will be done by those who occupy the premises. They need a foundation, an architectural design, and the tools to accomplish the job.

In *Fulfilling the Promises of Excellence*, one finds ideas and tools that teachers and administrators need as they respond to the external mandates for educational reform and improvement. The authors have borrowed from several literatures that are typically treated as independent. They enhance the philosophy of building from within rather than importing from outside. They offer options without imposing prescriptions. They recognize implicitly that practitioners themselves have a knowledge of how to proceed and build on their craft rather than on the abstract theories of the sciences. The reform movement of the 1980's provides a rare opportunity for educational practitioners. They have a mandate to broadcast their virtues, revitalize tired practices, relabel some strengths, and alter some weaknesses. Books like this will help them augment their own intuition with some general ideas and principles.

Terry Deal
Vanderbilt University, 1987

FULFILLING THE PROMISE OF EXCELLENCE—
A Practitioner's Guide to School Improvement

INTRODUCTION

Future historians will certainly point to 1983 as the year in which national attention was focused, once again, on the plight of U.S. public schools. The National Commission on Excellence in Education (1983, 5), fired one of the earliest salvos in what was to become a barrage of calls for school reform when it offered the following assessment of U.S. education:

> Our nation is at risk. Our once unchallenged preeminence in commerce, industry, science, and technological innovation is being over-taken by competitors throughout the world . . . . [T]he educational foundations of our society are presently being eroded by a rising tide of mediocrity that threatens our very future as a Nation and a people . . . . If an unfriendly foreign power had attempted to impose on America the mediocre educational performance that exists today, we might well have viewed it as an act of war . . . . We have, in effect, been committing an act of unthinking, unilateral educational disarmament.

Within two years of this report, over three hundred national and state task forces had investigated the condition of U.S. public schooling and offered a litany of advice. What has been the end result of these various calls for reform? Despite the fact that the *Nation at Risk* report described the condition of education as a crisis comparable to an act of war, there has been little response from the national government beyond exhortations. At the state level the legislative response has been generally to prescribe higher standards for students and teachers. Thus by 1985 forty-one states had shown their support for excellent schools by mandating that students take more courses in designated academic areas. In many states the requirements for teacher certification and tenure were raised, despite the fact that the National Center for Educational Statistics projects a critical shortage of teachers by the 1990s. Some studies, such as Mortimer Adler's *The Paideia Proposal* (1982), took a more pedagogical approach to the problems of schooling, calling for a massive overhauling of both the secondary school curriculum and the manner in which it is taught. Still others, such as Theodore Sizer's *A Review and Comment on the National Reports* (1984), called for a dramatic reduction in pupil-teacher ratios and replacement of the traditional, Carnegie-unit approach to graduation with the assessment of a portfolio of a student's work.

The response of practicing educators to these different reports, recommendations, and reforms has been reserved for several reasons. As John Casteen (1985), secretary of education of Virginia, observed, the education profession has not been a part of the excellence movement, a movement initiated and led by elected officials and business leaders and centered in state legislatures. As a result, educators have tended to view the excellence movement with the skepticism of outsiders. They have generally dismissed as simplistic solutions that focus on the manipulation of graduation requirements. Furthermore, practitioners are not in a position to enact proposals that call for massive increases in expenditures or the radical overhauling of the traditional curriculum of public schools. Thus they have dismissed those proposals as irrelevant to their immediate concerns of improving their schools. Even those who might have agreed with some of these recommendations for radical change were confronted with the compelling fact that the traditional U.S. school system represents one of this nation's most enduring institutions, and the likelihood of bringing about such change in the near future was remote at best.

An even greater concern to practitioners, however, was the fact that the excellence movement seemed to follow a regulatory strategy that mandated uniformity among schools at the same time as the research on effective schools was reporting that excellent schools tend to be self-directed and reasonably autonomous. Ernest Boyer (1985), president of the Carnegie Foundation for the Advancement of Teaching, expressed the concern that the vast majority of school reforms in the fifty states were centrally imposed. Chester Finn (1985, 65), assistant secretary of the United States Department of Education, summarized this dilemma when he wrote, "The excellence movement is trying to order schools to be better; and yet, the research shows that really good schools don't respond to orders. They can grow their own." In a report for the American Educational Studies Association, Raywid, Tesconi and Warren (1985, 14), were even more critical of the increasing reliance on rules and regulations, top-down formal systems, and detailed specifications of school practices that resulted from most of the school reform efforts:

[These] tendencies fly in the face of what we know about successful schools and about excellence in other types of organizations as well. In fact, the general strategy being adopted by most of the education reports, and being implemented now in a growing number of states, may be distinctly *opposed* to excellence.

Thus current practitioners have found little satisfaction in the excellence movement and continue to ask, "Given the existing structure and purpose of American education, what can I do to improve my school; what can I do to move my school toward excellence?"

We believe that the answer to this question will not be found in the admonishment of a national report or the mandate of a state legislature. We concur with Karen Seashore Lewis (1986, 35), of Harvard University, who examined research studies of European, Japanese, and American public schools and concluded: "Our best bet for improving schools lies not with fine tuning state reforms . . .but with stimulating individual schools to change and providing them with assistance." This book is intended for those practitioners—boards of education, superintendents, principals, and teachers—who are working at the local level to improve schools one building or one district at a time. It is also aimed at the colleges and universities that seek to prepare current and future teachers and administrators to be positive change agents in the schools in which they work. The book offers specific, practical recommendations on how to create an excellent school.

In developing recommendations we have attempted to integrate two important bodies of research that have emerged over the past decade. The first is the research on effective schools. The work of Ron Edmonds, George Weber, Michael Rutter, Wilbur Brookover, Larry Lezotte, and others has established that schools do indeed make a difference, and that some are much more effective than others. This research also has identified certain characteristics consistently found in effective schools. Many of the recommendations that we offer are based on the findings of this body of work.

The second area of research that we draw upon includes the studies of effective business practices and the leadership behind those practices. In August of 1986 Secretary of Education William Bennett (1986, 11), suggested that America's schools be run like small businesses. If a company produces shoddy products or provides poor services, Bennett argued, it is soon out of business. He called for schools to be held similarly accountable. Bennett concluded this analogy between business and education with the pronouncement, "If schools can't deliver what the public wants, they should be shut down." We note the inescapable irony in a call for greater productivity, service, and accountability from a member of an administration overseeing a budget with a deficit approaching $250 billion. Furthermore, we do not concur with the notion that schools should be subjected to some form of educational social Darwinism to eliminate those that are less fit. We do believe, however, that the current studies of the philosophy, policies, and procedures of outstanding American companies and those who lead them offer much to anyone interested in improving schools.

We recognize that there are important differences between the worlds of business and education. The education of a child is not equivalent to the production of an automobile. The inputs in the world of education are infinitely more complex than those in the world of work. A failed experiment in the schooling of children cannot be written off to research and development with the same nonchalance that business can apply to an unsuccessful product line. Most important, the bottom line of educational effectiveness is far more shadowy and elusive than the measures industry uses to evaluate its success. These differences should be neither ignored nor minimized. Nevertheless, we remain convinced that works such as *In Search of Excellence* by Thomas Peters and Robert Waterman (1982), *Leaders* by Warren Bennis and Burt Nanus (1985), *Reinventing the Corporation* by John Naisbitt and Patricia Aburdene (1985), *Peak Performers* by Charles Garfield (1986), *The Change Masters* by Rosabeth Moss Kanter (1983), *Corporate Cultures* by Terrence Deal and Allan Kennedy (1982), and *A Passion for Excellence* by Thomas Peters and Nancy Austin (1985), are rich with ideas and information that school practitioners would do well to apply to the school setting. Unfortunately, educators have tended to overlook the important lessons that can be learned from the study of organizations outside of education. We have attempted to overcome this tendency by merging the research on effective business practices with the research on effective schools and providing specific examples of how the concepts of each can be applied in a school.

This book also represents a merger of another kind, a merger of theory and practice. Too often educational researchers and educational practitioners live in different worlds, hold different interests, and speak different languages. This book, written by a dean of a college of education whose background is in research and by a principal of an outstanding high school, attempts to bridge the chasm between theory and practice. We have reviewed the research, but we have also interviewed principals from a number of nationally recognized schools to gain further insights into the actual practices that move a school toward excellence. The suggestions we offer for school improvement are both based on research and proven in practice.

The findings from the diverse sources we consulted—research on effective schools, studies of outstanding businesses, analyses of leadership, and the specific practices and procedures of a number of fine schools—were remarkably consistent. Thus we are able to offer the following observations to those interested in moving a school toward excellence.

1. *Excellent schools have a clear vision of what they are attempting to accomplish, what they are trying to become.* Effective organizations have a vision that provides a sense of purpose, direction, and ideal future state to those within the organization. All too often, schools lack such vision. In his study for the Carnegie Foundation, Ernest Boyer (1983, 63), concluded: "High schools lack a clear and vital mission. They are unable to find common purposes or establish educational priorities that are widely shared. They seem unable to put it all together. The institution is adrift." Raywid, Tesconi and Warren (1985, 9), contend that *"the articulation of an overall purpose for the public schools is the most important educational challenge of the day."* The mandate that a school become "excellent" does little to provide the vision that schools so desperately need. What is an excellent school? Is it one in which there are many National Merit Scholars, one in which a high per-

centage of graduates go on to college, one in which all students achieve a specified minimum competency regardless of race, or one in which the drop-out rate is low? Is the definition of an excellent school the same in an affluent suburb as it is in a rural community or in the inner city? As Chester Finn (1985, 65) observed, "If you can't decide what an ideal system looks like, you can't create policies to get there." Chapter One discusses the importance of establishing a vision to guide a school's improvement effort and offers a process for arriving at this articulated vision.

2. *The day-to-day operation of an excellent school is guided by a few shared central values.* Effective organizations have shared values that reflect the vision of the organization. These values help individuals to understand how they are expected to behave and serve as a mechanism for sanctioning or proscribing behavior. Furthermore, because they reflect certain parameters and standards, the values enable individuals to exercise greater autonomy. The identification, communication, and shaping of central values is a key to the success of an excellent school. Chapter Two identifies several ways in which the values of a school can be formulated and emphasized.

3. *Excellent schools have principals who are effective leaders.* The importance of strong leadership has been cited again and again in both the studies of excellent businesses and the research on effective schools. But what is a strong leader—one with vision who insists that things be done a certain way or one who empowers others by providing them with both responsibility and autonomy? Effective principals

must be able to do both. They must be forceful and aggressive promoters and protectors of the values of their schools and at the same time provide their teachers with the freedom and autonomy to satisfy personal and professional needs. They must be strong instructional leaders and, at the same time, encourage teachers to assume more and more responsibility for instructional matters. Chapter Three suggests that a principal need not choose between being a strong leader and empowering teachers and offers a framework for acting as both an autocratic defender of values and a champion of teacher autonomy.

4. *Excellent schools have principals who are attentive managers of climate.* Although discussions of school climate are often restricted to the degree of satisfaction expressed by students and staff, the excellent school considers climate a function of both satisfaction and productivity (that is, student achievement). A safe and orderly atmosphere is essential to the pursuit of excellence. In the excellent schools expectations for student behavior are based on a few general guidelines or values, and steps are taken to ensure that students are aware of those values. Students are provided with positive incentives for appropriate behavior. The entire staff accepts responsibility for enforcing the disciplinary values of the school and responds promptly and consistently to students who ignore them. Furthermore, excellent schools establish an ecology of high expectations or sense of academic press that affects both students and teachers. Finally, the principal keeps a finger on the pulse of the climate of the school by using a variety of strategies to keep in touch. Chapter Four

discusses the characteristics of positive school climate and how principals can influence climate in a beneficial way.

5. *The curriculum of an excellent school reflects the values of the school and provides a focus that helps teachers and students "stick to the knitting."* In order to ensure a sharp focus within the organization, many successful companies operate according to the premise that "to have more than one goal is to have no goals at all." Schools, on the other hand, tend to suffer from curriculum overload. The curricula of most schools seem to advise teachers to pay attention to everything. Excellent schools develop and offer a curriculum that reflects or fits the values of the school and helps to focus the attention of teachers and students on what learning is considered most significant. Chapter Five offers a process for curriculum development and suggests criteria for assessing the curriculum of a school.

6. *Excellent schools promote excellence in teaching.* Many of the proposals that have resulted from the educational reform movement seem designed to provide "teacher proof schools." As Raywid, Tesconi, and Warren (1985, 14) observed, "The most discussed of the recent education reports link excellence to insurance against teaching judgments." We believe that it is self-evident that a school will only be as effective or as good as the teaching that takes place within it. Thus the quality of teaching is a major concern in an excellent school. The quality of teaching is determined by (a) the accuracy, adequacy, and relevance of the content; (b) the teacher's technical skills in such areas as planning, clarity, questioning strategies, classroom management, etc.;

and (c) those interpersonal characteristics of a teacher that affect classroom climate. Chapter Six provides a three part model for considering teaching and presents a review of the current research on effective teaching.

7. *Excellent schools monitor what is important.* Studies of effective leaders consistently conclude that these leaders communicate what the organization values by monitoring or paying attention to the factors that reflect those values. Robert Waterman (1985, 266), went so far as to say that the *only* way a leader can influence an organization is by paying attention to what is significant: "Attention is all there is." We believe that an excellent school expresses its values by monitoring the curriculum, student achievement, and teaching. Chapter Seven provides processes for monitoring each of these three areas and offers a teacher supervision model that is designed to both improve instruction and empower teachers.

8. *Excellent schools celebrate the presence of their core values with ceremonies and rituals.* Effective businesses create systems that are specifically designed to produce lots of winners and to celebrate winning once it occurs. These celebrations recognize and promote the values upheld by the company. Deal and Kennedy concluded that such ritualization and celebration of values is essential to the survival of an organization. The celebration of values is an area that has generally been neglected by public schools. Educators have been quick to advise parents of failure and slow to recognize success. Rituals and celebrations have tended to focus on athletic accomplishment or personal popularity rather than academic achievement or exemplary effort. Chapter

Eight describes how schools can promote their core values by paying attention to celebration and rituals.

9. *Excellent schools sustain their commitment to improvement through systematic self-renewal.* Excellent schools are never satisfied. Although those who work in an excellent school may take considerable pride in its achievements, they realize that the pursuit of excellence is a process that never results in a final product—it is a journey rather than a destination. This realization results in a commitment to continual renewal. If staff members require training and/or coaching to advance the values of the school, that training is provided. As long-term improvement plans run their course, new plans are developed to promote improvement in other areas of the school operation. Most important, the vision of excellence is pursued relentlessly. These schools stay the course. Chapter Nine identifies barriers to organizational change, offers suggestions as to how those barriers might be overcome, and discusses the conditions that are associated with positive change and innovation. Finally, it calls upon those interested in school improvement to commit themselves and their schools to perpetual renewal.

We anticipate that there will be readers who dismiss this list of the characteristics of an excellent school as idealistic. These individuals will want to know what can be done to achieve excellence in the "real world" of a particular school if its teachers are unable to agree on central values, or the principal is an ineffective leader, or procedures are not in place to monitor the curriculum. Our response is twofold. First, we make no apologies for offering an ideal, for it is the vision of an ideal that inspires people and organizations to make the extraordinary effort and commitment necessary to achieve excellence. Second, although we are convinced that the absence of any one of the characteristics we have described lessens the likelihood that a given school will achieve excellence, we believe that every step in the direction of excellence is a worthwhile one.

In the final analysis, perhaps the most essential ingredient in the creation of an excellent school is the desire of those within it to make the school excellent. Peters and Austin concluded that it takes guts and commitment to pursue excellence, and both of these characteristics depend on desire. It is hoped that this book will provide both encouragement and practical advice for those who have that desire. Over 150 years ago the English author Issac D'Israeli (1834, 417) observed, "It is a wretched waste to be gratified with mediocrity when the excellent lies before us." The path to excellence is available to those educators who have the determination to pursue it with tenacity. May the suggestions in this book speed their journey.

CHAPTER ONE

Developing A Shared Vision Of An Excellent School

If there is a spark of genius in the leadership function at all it must be in this transcending ability, a kind of magic, to assemble—out of all the variety of images, signals, forecasts and alternatives—a clearly articulated vision of the future that is at once single, easily understood, clearly desirable, and energizing.

Warren Bennis and Burt Nanus, (1985, 103) *Leaders*

I have discussed these matters with a great variety of individuals and groups throughout the country, and I find that "excellence" is a curiously powerful word—a word about which people feel strongly and deeply. But it is a word that means different things to different people. It is a little like those ink blots that psychologists use to interpret personality. As the individual contemplates the word "excellence" he reads into it his own aspirations, his own conception of high stan-

1

dards, his hopes for a better world. And it brings powerfully to his mind evidence of the betrayal of excellence (as he conceives it). He thinks not only of the greatness we might achieve but of the mediocrity we have fallen into.

John W. Gardner, (1961, xii) *Excellence*

What do excellent organizations have in common? What characterizes an excellent school? Where do we begin once we have decided to move toward excellence in schooling? These are tough questions, but not impossible ones. Recent research on school effectiveness has generated a much sharper picture of what an effective school looks like, and recent research on organizational behavior and leadership has added a new dimension to what we know about excellent organizations. One thing seems clear: Excellent organizations have a shared sense of purpose, a direction, or—as Warren Bennis and Burt Nanus put it—a shared vision.

How many teachers have felt the frustration of teaching year after year in a school in which the overriding concern seems to be maintaining the status quo? Get the school open. Make it to Christmas, then spring break. After spring break it is not long until school is out and another year is gone. How many teachers have felt the disappointment of never being a part of anything grand and exciting related to their work? Schools do not have to be merely a collection of teachers, all "doing their own thing." Schools can be (and in many instances are) organizations with an overriding purpose and a sense of shared commitment. Such schools have a sense of identity and a view of the future. A shared vision of the future is synonymous with a healthy organization. It is the framework around which an excellent school is developed.

2

DESCRIBING THE SCHOOL YOU SEEK TO BECOME

About the same time as *A Nation at Risk* was capturing headlines with its gloomy assessment of U.S. education, a small school district in the northern suburbs of Chicago announced a vacancy in the principalship of the high school. As the final step in the selection process for that position, candidates went through a series of separate interviews with the board of education, the administrators of the district, a faculty committee, and a student committee. The interview process allowed for the free exchange of questions and answers. One of the candidates took advantage of that opportunity to ask each of the four groups to describe the biggest challenge facing the new principal. Although the question was asked of each group independently, the answers were remarkably consistent. Board members, administrators, teachers, and students all expressed the belief that their school had the potential to be an excellent school, and the major task facing the new principal was to lead the school in realizing that potential. The candidate who had raised the question was ultimately selected, and he accepted the position with the clear understanding that his charge was to create an excellent public school.

Meanwhile, incumbent administrators were receiving similar directives in schools throughout the United States. *A Nation at Risk* and a host of other reports had fueled public interest in education. The Carnegie Foundation report (1986) entitled *High School: A Report on Secondary Education in America* was just one of many that urged school boards and state legislatures to commit their schools to excellence. Every high school in the nation should "take steps to achieve excellence," advised

3

the Carnegie report, and across the country local boards of education presented their administrators with the mandate to create an excellent school.

Administrators all over the country could be encouraged by the fact that there seemed to be a real consensus on the goal of achieving excellence. Sincere people in various roles in the school community seemed to genuinely endorse that goal for their school. After all, who could be anti-excellence? Thus the question facing these administrators was how to capitalize on this consensus in order to implement policies to create an excellent school. At the high school level, all too often their response to this opportunity began and ended with discussion of recommendations to increase graduation requirements. Local boards of education and state legislatures reasoned that increasing the number of years that students were required to study English, mathematics, science, computer science, and social studies would present a clear statement of the high expectations and lofty goals of a school district. The corresponding recommendation at the elementary level called for more emphasis on these core academic subjects and less on everything else.

But excellence, like beauty, is in the eye of the beholder. Once increased attention to particular subjects has been mandated, the drive to create an excellent school often stalls. The fact that disparate groups might endorse the general concept of an excellent school does not necessarily provide a district with either a meaningful consensus or a clearly defined goal. Various board members, veteran teachers, school administrators, and high school students probably all have their own concepts of an excellent school. A district is not provided with a useful self-image if it makes no attempt to move the concept of an excellent school from the general to the specific. A goal as vague as achieving excellence fails to give direction or purpose to a school or its personnel. As Chester Finn (1985, 65) observed, "If you can't decide what an ideal system would look like, you can't create policies to get there." Before the drive for excellence can progress, differences in opinions within or between the groups that comprise a school's population as to what constitutes an excellent school must be resolved.

The critical importance of vision has been cited by those who have studied effective businesses and effective leaders. In *Reinventing the Corporation* (1985, 24) John Naisbitt and Patricia Aburdene conclude that the first ingredient in establishing an outstanding company is a "powerful vision, a whole new sense of where a company is going and how to get there." In their highly regarded study of leadership, Warren Bennis and Burt Nanus (1985, 89) explained that vision "articulates a view of a realistic, credible, attractive future for the organization, a condition that is better in some important ways than what now exists. A vision is a target that beckons." Thus it is the shared vision that provides an organization with a sense of purpose, direction, and ideal future state. In order to be in a position to work toward the ideal it has described, a community must (1) define a vision that provides a sense of mission for its schools and (2) win broad support for that vision. The development of a process that results in both this common vision of an excellent school and wide-spread support for the vision is where the quest for excellence should begin.

The Benefits of Establishing a Statement of Excellence

Several benefits accrue to the district that completes the process of describing the school it wishes to provide.

The first is in the subtle but significant area of attitude. Excellence in any field is unattainable unless someone has the will, the desire, or, as Tom Peters and Nancy Austin described it, the "passion" to achieve great things. This process results in a public pronouncement that a particular district is committed to the lofty goal of achieving excellence. There is a heightened awareness of that goal on the part of the various publics that comprise a district, and those who embrace the goal have a focal point around which to rally. As Naisbitt and Aburdene (1985, 27) said, "When people have a vision they are motivated to make it a reality." In his study of peak performers in business, Charles Garfield found that the one characteristic always present in these achievers is a vision that fuels their motivation. Psychologists tell us that one of our most basic human needs is the need to feel useful, to feel we are engaged in significant, purposeful endeavor. George Bernard Shaw (1973, 84) captured that need when he wrote, "This is the true joy of life, the being used for a purpose recognized by yourself as a mighty one." A compelling vision of what a school can be provides the "mighty purpose" that both motivates the members of a school community and enables them to fulfill their personal needs.

A second major benefit of completing this process is the direction it gives to individuals within the organization. As Bennis and Nanus pointed out, if an organization has a clear sense of its purpose, direction, and ideal future state, its members are able to find and understand their roles within that organization. When members of the school community understand the mission statement for their school, some very clear guidelines for their own conduct begin to emerge. These guidelines can be explicitly enumerated to provide a concise statement of the core values or principles that each group will be expected to observe. Further explanation and examples of this procedure will be provided in Chapter Two.

A third benefit of describing the ideal school is that it helps a school establish an agenda for action. As Naisbitt and Aburdene observed (1985, 27), "It is easier to get from point A to point B if you know where point B is and how to recognize it when you have arrived." Once a description exists, current policies, practices, and conditions can be evaluated to identify any discrepancies between the reality of the existing school and the characteristics of the ideal school that has been described.

Sometimes this evaluation will bring to light practices or policies of individuals that need to be changed. For example, the principal in one school that completed this process found a glaring discrepancy between the standard of the school and one teacher's grading practices. When the community drafted its description of an excellent school, which was eventually adopted by the board of education as district policy, it included the notion that teachers were to have high expectations for all students, including the expectation that every student could master the course objectives. One teacher had a long-standing practice of adding the total number of points each student had earned during the semester and then applying the bell-shaped curve to the continuum of students' scores. Of course this practice meant that a certain number of her students were preordained to fail the course each semester. When the principal pointed out the discrepancy to the teacher, the teacher's initial reaction was to allege that her academic freedom was being violated. But when her colleagues, who had endorsed the description of an excellent school, refused to side with her, she agreed to change her practice.

The description can also be used to assess school-wide policies and practices. One district described an excellent high school as one in which a prescribed curriculum followed by all students ensured a common core of learning. This statement was clearly not consistent with the graduation requirements of the school, which allowed students to elect nearly 50 percent of their courses and put virtually no restrictions on their choices. A task force was asked to recommend revisions in graduation requirements to make them more consistent with the standard established in the description of the excellent school. This task force ultimately recommended changes that allowed students to elect only one-third of their courses and ensured the distribution of these electives over a number of different areas.

USING RESEARCH AS A BASIS FOR DEVELOPING A FRAMEWORK FOR EXCELLENCE

In defining the school you seek, it is important to recognize the contribution research can play in describing an excellent school. Although research findings do not provide all the answers we need regarding school excellence, they can provide a practitioner with a frame of reference for thinking about characteristics that seem essential for effective schooling. Research findings should be viewed not as a simple recipe for improvement, but rather as a theoretical framework around which an excellent school can be developed.

The School Effectiveness Research

In keeping with the fact that excellence is in the eye of the beholder, ideas about excellence—particularly excel-

8

lence in schooling—change periodically. Traditionally, measures of excellence in schooling have emphasized such factors as college degrees earned by the faculty, class size, the number of library books, and the adequacy of the facility. These aspects of schooling still form the basic criteria for most school accreditation programs.

Periodically in the history of education, the effectiveness of schooling has been equated with the degree to which students were prepared to enter the world of work. This emphasis has usually surfaced during periods of high unemployment and a slow down in the economy. During such times the focus has been on vocational education, career education, and career counseling.

During the late 1960s and the 1970s, the prevailing attitude within the research community was that, by and large, schools made very little difference in student achievement. *The Coleman Report, Racial Isolation in the Public Schools*, and *Disequality* are but a few of the studies that gave support to the idea that the socioeconomic status of children's families was responsible, more than any other factor, for student achievement. This led to the notion that since schools could not do very much to affect student achievement, an excellent school was one that created an atmosphere where kids enjoyed school and learned to feel good about themselves.

In 1979 Michael Rutter and others published results that directly challenged the assumption that schools make very little difference in student achievement. Although a few studies done as early as 1974 had examined schooling practices and academic achievement, Rutter's *Fifteen Thousand Hours: Secondary Schools and Their Effects on Children* (1979) brought this issue to the forefront. Additional studies by Brookover and Lezotte (1979) and Phi Delta Kappa (1980)

9

supported Rutter's findings. Ron Edmonds' (1979) re-search on school effectiveness may have contributed more than any other study to the widespread recognition that what schools do, *does* affect the achievement of students. Edmonds' conclusions may seem rather obvi-ous at first glance, but they use findings consistent with those of the previously mentioned studies to effectively refute ideas that had become prevalent in the seventies.

What does the research on school effectiveness tell us about excellent schools? There are many excellent syn-theses of the research findings available, but among the best is one done by the Northwest Regional Educational Laboratory (1984) in Portland, Oregon. This synthesis, focusing on research studies that identified schooling practices and characteristics associated with measurable improvements in student achievement and behavior, provides the following picture of an effective school.

1. Everyone emphasizes the importance of learning.
2. Strong leadership guides the instructional program.
3. The curriculum is based on clear goals and objec-tives.
4. Students are grouped to promote effective instruc-tion.
5. School time is used for learning.
6. Learning progress is monitored closely.
7. Discipline is firm and consistent.
8. There are high expectations for quality instruction.
9. Incentives and rewards are used to build strong motivation.
10. Parents are invited to become involved.
11. Teachers and administrators continually strive to improve instructional effectiveness.
12. There are pleasant conditions for learning.

Stewart Purkey and Marshall Smith (1983) conducted a review of the research on school effectiveness as of 1982 and identified what they believe are the most important characteristics of effective schools. Purkey and Smith grouped characteristics into two categories: (1) organizational and structural variables and (2) process-form variables. The organizational and structural variables include:

- school site management
- leadership
- staff stability
- curriculum articulation and organization
- staff development
- parental involvement and support
- school wide recognition of academic success
- maximized learning time
- district support

The process-form variables associated with school effectiveness are:

- collaborative planning and collegial relationships
- sense of community
- clear goals and high expectations that are commonly shared
- order and discipline

11

Researchers may disagree about a particular finding or a particular research methodology, but research on effective schools does provide a surprisingly clear and consistent picture of school practices and characteristics associated with student achievement. Thus, although the findings are not a recipe for quick success, they do form a useful framework for thinking about and planning for school improvement.

Research from America's Best-Run Companies

Obviously, student learning is what schools are all about. Increasing student achievement scores, however, is but one characteristic of an excellent school. What about other aspects of organizational life? What about student and faculty morale—a sense of pride and dedication? These issues are relevant to all organizations, and schools are no exception. We believe that many of the findings from studies outside of education are as applicable to schools as they are to business. Research findings on such topics as organizational climate, organizational effectiveness, personnel development, leadership, and organizational change provide a portrait of a healthy, vital organization.

One of the most widely read descriptions of common characteristics of excellent companies is *In Search of Excellence* (1982) by Tom Peters and Robert Waterman. This study of the factors that have contributed to the success of America's best-run companies is rich with information on leadership and organizational climate that can readily be applied to schools. The ideas in this book and others like it should be made available to those attempting to describe an excellent school. These ideas can serve as an effective catalyst for discussions of those characteristics other than academic achievement that are important ingredients of excellence. A brief summary of the conclusions reached by Peters and Waterman is presented below. Specific applications of their findings to the school setting will be discussed throughout this book.

1. *The best run companies show a bias for action, for getting things done.* Excellent companies get quick action because their organizations are fluid. "These companies are characterized by a vast network of informal, open communications. . . . The right people get into contact with each other regularly. . . . [There is] a virtual technology of keeping in touch" (1982, 121-23).

2. *The best companies stick close to the customer.* Excellent companies learn from the people they serve. These companies are good listeners and get many of their best ideas from their customers.

3. *Excellent companies encourage autonomy and entrepreneurship.* Outstanding companies foster many leaders and innovators throughout the organization. Managers in these companies do not launch a new project unless an individual zealot or champion volunteers to embrace that project and becomes personally committed to its success.

4. *The best run companies achieve productivity through people.* Managers in excellent companies realize that a prime motivational factor is the individual's perception that he or she is doing well. Consequently these companies set goals that most people can reach and let employees know when they are doing well.

These firms celebrate success with ceremony and hoopla.

5. *The best companies are hands-on, value-driven organizations.* In excellent companies top management stays close to the action—walking plant floors, visiting stores, and so on. These leaders believe in "management by walking about." And they continually remind employees of the organization's values and mission.

6. *Excellent companies stick to their knitting.* The best-run companies stay with the basics rather than diversifying their goals or tasks.

7. *The best run companies maintain a simple form and a lean staff.* The best run corporations have a structure that is "elegantly simple." Top level staffs are lean.

8. *Excellent companies are simultaneously "loose" and "tight."* Even as they encourage individual initiative and autonomy ("looseness"), the best companies also demand rigid adherence ("tightness") to a few core values that drive and give direction to everyone in the organization.

REACHING A CONSENSUS

The ultimate value of a school's definition or vision of excellence will depend not on its format but on whether it elicits feelings of ownership and endorsement from the various groups in the school district. School leaders who feel certain of the direction they want their schools to take and who are impatient to initiate school improvement may be tempted to draft a personal mission statement for their schools and present it as a fait accompli.

That temptation should be resisted. Bennis and Nanus (1985, 105) insist that if an organization is to be successful, it must be guided by a vision that has grown from the needs of the entire organization and is claimed or owned by all important actors. Effective leaders recognize that vision cannot be established by edict or coercion. In their study of outstanding business leaders, Bennis and Nanus found that although the leader may have been the one to articulate and focus attention on a particular vision, he or she was rarely the one who conceived of the vision in the first place. The leaders were great askers and great listeners. They were able to synthesize a vision that reflected the needs of those in the organization because they involved the members of the organization in the process of formulating that vision.

Successful principals understand that the involvement of appropriate people in a consensus decision-making process will have an important influence on the degree of commitment to achieving excellence in the school. Involvement leads to the feeling that the definition of excellence is one's own rather than the principal's. Too often teachers are asked to commit themselves to someone else's notions about what they should value. In many schools, when a new direction is introduced, the attitude of the teachers is "Be patient, play the game, this too shall pass!" If teachers, administrators, and parents are to be genuinely committed to achieving an excellent school, they must play an important part in reaching a consensus about the school they seek to provide.

Obviously, involving a variety of people in a consensus decision-making process is difficult, time-consuming, and often frustrating. Disagreements will arise, time will be wasted, and there will be moments when things seem to come to a standstill. At such times, the principal must provide the leadership necessary to maintain the group's cohesiveness and move the process along. The principal must realize that it is much better to resolve controversial issues during this early stage of the school improvement process than to wait and have them coming up repeatedly during the day-to-day operation of the school.

Now for a word of caution. Since working with groups in reaching consensus is a very difficult and time-consuming task, there is a tendency for the principal to turn this job over to someone else—perhaps a supervisor, a consultant, or a professor from a nearby university. Although this approach may be less trying, it has some very real problems that will manifest themselves in the long run. A most important point to remember is this: Faculty, parents and students look to the principal of the school for leadership. The principal's ideas, values, likes, and dislikes are important to people. They believe, although they may not say so, that ultimately the principal's view will carry the most weight anyway. Hence it is important for the principal to work *with* groups and demonstrate genuine interest and resolve by taking an active and viable role in the consensus process.

Establishing a Committee for Excellence

One way to address the issue of reaching a consensus about what constitutes an excellent school is to establish a committee for excellence. The committee can not only reach an agreement about the major characteristics of an excellent school, but can also provide input for the school improvement plan. The composition of this committee and its ability to achieve consensus can be the major factors in determining the general support for a school improvement effort. Thus the question of who will serve on the committee is a critical one. It is a mistake to simply invite volunteers; membership on the committee is too important to be left to chance. Those initiating the school improvement effort should identify key individuals to be invited to serve on the committee. The following factors should be taken into consideration:

1. *The diverse groups within the school district should be represented.* The committee should include representatives of the major groups that form a school community—teachers, parents, administrators, students, community members, business leaders, etc. Since the main responsibility for implementing a school improvement plan will generally fall on teachers, they should be heavily represented on the committee.

2. *The individuals chosen should be influential within the groups they represent.* Every faculty, every student body, and every community include highly regarded individuals who are able to influence opinion within their group. These key actors should be identified and encouraged to participate on the committee.

3. *Committee members must be able to maintain a broad perspective.* Members of the committee must have the capacity to examine ideas and proposals in terms of their total impact on the school. They also must be able to consider and appreciate different points of view. The committee is no place for single-issue zealots who are unwilling to compromise.

4. *Key policymakers must be included.* Nothing will extinguish enthusiasm for the effort to create an

17

excellent school more quickly than the refusal of policymakers to enact the proposals of the committee after it has arrived at a consensus. Therefore, it is highly advisable to include one of the key decision makers of the school on this committee. A superintendent, principal, or influential member of the board of education can caution the committee if it begins to exceed the parameters of its mission and can help win final approval for recommendations.

Success in building consensus will depend to a great degree on the interpersonal and communications skills of the principal. The principal must be skilled in group processes and consensus building. If the committee resorts to simple majority rule to arrive at decisions, there will inevitably be winners and losers on every issue. This, in turn, will make it more difficult to win broad support for the final product of the committee. It is unlikely that each member of the group will support every decision as the very best available option. Nevertheless, it is the responsibility of the principal to keep an issue before the group until it has reached a decision that all members agree to support.

At the initial meeting of the committee, the principal should help the group define its purpose. Subsequent misunderstandings and misdirected efforts are less likely if the committee agrees to a succinct statement of purpose at the outset. Some advocates of the consensus process argue that this statement of purpose should emerge from the initial discussions of the committee. However, the purpose or charge of the committee should have already been defined, at least in general terms, by the school district. Therefore, the leader can expedite the work of the committee if he or she presents a tentative statement of purpose as a basis for discussion. The leader can then demonstrate the consensus process for decision making as the group considers this statement.

Once the group has agreed to a statement of purpose and understands the consensus building process that it will try to follow in making decisions, the leader should present the group with a concise summary of the key findings of the research on effective schools. This research has been remarkably consistent in identifying the characteristics of effective schools, and members of the committee should have the benefit of its findings. This brief review of research, presented in nontechnical terms, will also ensure some common background information for members who will undoubtedly come to the committee with very different levels of knowledge of school practices.

Next the committee must decide how it will proceed with its task. As strategies are developed, the leader should remind the committee that general support for its final recommendations is best fostered by engaging the different segments of the school community in discussion of the type of school they would like to have in that community. The ultimate goal of the committee should be to arrive at a description of an excellent school that teachers, parents, students, and community members will endorse. If the committee is able to extend its own consensus approach to decision making to each of these groups, it will promote the sense of ownership in the final product that is necessary to achieve that ultimate goal.

Gaining Consensus: A Process

There are any number of techniques or processes one can use to gain consensus about important issues. One relatively simple yet effective approach combines the technique of brainstorming with a process for reaching consensus. Principals can use this process with their own faculty in order to reach a consensus about the characteristics of an excellent school.

The first step is to brainstorm the characteristics that participants believe are essential to an excellent school. Characteristics are simply recorded on a chalkboard as they are generated. At this point no comments about the relative merit of the ideas are allowed. After the ideas have been listed on the board, the next step is to consolidate similar characteristics. One school group that went through this process came up with the following consolidated list:

- Academic achievement

- Quality teaching

- Concern for students' feelings, emotions, and attitudes

- High morale and a sense of pride among the faculty and students

- Concern for students' physical and social development

- Quality of facilities

- Warmth and humor

After the consolidated list has been generated, the participants should discuss, usually in small groups, the merits of each characteristic. Each group should rank order the items in the list from the most essential to the least essential. Voting should not be allowed. Rather, the groups should reach a consensus that each member of the group can support.

There are many ways to finalize the choice of characteristics. One way that has proven successful is to have each group present its prioritized list to the larger group and then attach a posterboard copy of the list to the wall with masking tape. After all the lists have been presented and explained, each participant is given ten votes to cast for the characteristics he or she feels are most important. (Voting can be done either by making marks on the lists or by attaching stick on stars.) Participants may cast all of their votes for one characteristic, or they may distribute their votes over a number of ideas.

After the votes have been tabulated, a statement describing the characteristics of an excellent school is written in narrative form. This step is normally carried out between meetings. The draft statement is then discussed and refined at subsequent meetings until it is acceptable to the entire group.

Once the committee has completed its final draft and won the approval of the board of education for its description of an excellent school, the major work of the committee is finished. Generally, the board of education will assume the responsibility for overseeing a school improvement plan to address the discrepancies between existing conditions in the school and the ideal that has been described. It is also the responsibility of the board to make the public aware of the district's description of an excellent school. The description itself should be disseminated at every opportunity, not only at the time of adoption through press releases and school mailings to the community, but also on an ongoing basis through prominent display in parent handbooks, faculty manuals, and student handbooks.

21

This process can be adapted to fit various situations. It can be simplified for smaller groups. Successful use of the technique with larger, more heterogenous groups will require more work and planning. But regardless of the complexity of the process, the essential idea is this: Reaching a consensus on what an excellent school looks like and what the school seeks to become is the first step, and a crucial step, in achieving excellence.

DEVELOPING A DEFINITION OF EXCELLENCE: A CASE IN POINT

The activities of a school district in suburban Chicago provide a good example of the process just described. The school district appointed a committee to consider what steps could be taken to encourage the pursuit of excellence in the area high school. The Committee on Excellence, as it was called, was chaired by the principal and included three parents, three teachers, a representative of the business community, and two students. At its first meetings the committee reviewed the findings of several different studies of effective schools in order to ensure some common background and common vocabulary. The committee then outlined the steps it would follow in completing its charge.

The first step was to ask a number of different groups to discuss the question, "What are the characteristics of an excellent school?" The principal and a member of the committee met with staff members, first in sessions of ten or twelve and then as a group, to explore the question. Teachers led discussions in their homerooms and student members of the committee recorded the results. Discussions were held with the members of the parent-teacher organization, athletic booster club, band and choral booster clubs, and the parent advisory boards for each academic area. Coffees were held in the community, the Rotarians and the Lions devoted an afternoon to the topic, and representatives of business and industry responded to an invitation to spend a morning discussing their views of an excellent school. The decision to conduct this series of discussions rather than to survey these groups through the mail turned out to be a fortunate one. Not only did participants have the benefit of one another's ideas, but the scores of discussions going on throughout the school district focused the attention of the entire community on education. Most important, the board of education's interest in and commitment to providing an excellent school was demonstrated in a very public way.

After spending several weeks conducting discussions, the Committee on Excellence began to compile a list of the characteristics identified by the different groups. The members of the committee were struck by the similarities. Teachers, administrators, parents, students, and community members were remarkably consistent in their conclusions. Using these results, the committee proceeded to write the description of an excellent school. Despite the consensus, the committee found that it had to consider each group's conclusions carefully as it wrote its description. When the initial draft was completed, committee members went back to the various constituencies to share the description. Each group was invited to suggest revisions, deletions, and additions. The committee then considered these various recommendations as it prepared the final draft of its report.

Two months after the committee had been given its

charge by the board of education, it presented the board with a composite description of an excellent school. Two months later the board of education took formal action to adopt that description as the standard to be achieved and maintained in the school district. The description is presented here in its entirety.

Maintenance of Standards of Excellence

The Board of Education and staff have as a primary goal the maintenance of our school as an excellent school. Both the Board and staff shall be guided in that effort by standards or characteristics agreed to be evident in an excellent school. Those are as follows:

I. PEOPLE

An excellent school is the outgrowth of a Board of Education, administration, staff, parents, students, and community, all of whom share the goal of excellence for that school. In such a school: The staff is characterized by the following (not listed in order of importance):

1. Professionalism
2. Motivation
3. Enthusiasm
4. Compassion
5. Creativity
6. Dedication
7. Integrity
8. Morality
9. Staff members possess expertise in their curricular areas and in teaching technique, as well as expertise

in their cocurricular and extracurricular assignments.
10. The faculty is recognized as the heart of the excellent school, and its commitment to excellence is acknowledged by all.
11. The Principal is an active member of the school community and as such provides instructional leadership.
12. Parents play an active role in the education of their children.
13. The Board of Education and its administrative officers facilitate the educational process through informed decision making.
14. Community/parental support for the school is evident by their willingness to serve on advisory committees, booster groups and task forces, by attendance at cocurricular and extracurricular events, by participation at special events, etc.
15. The administrative structure enhances the educational process.

II. RELATIONSHIPS

An excellent school is characterized by an atmosphere of mutual respect and consideration among all members of the school community—students, staff, parents, administrators, Board members and community members. In such a school:

1. Open communication exists among students, staff, parents, administrators and the Board of Education.
2. Students, staff and community feel a sense of ownership and pride in the school.

3. The Principal is visible and accessible to students and faculty and, within reason, takes part in the daily activities of the school.
4. Parents and faculty work together to emphasize the value of education and to monitor the academic performance of students.

III. OPPORTUNITIES

Curricular

An excellent school provides all students with an opportunity to pursue a course of study that enables them to become productive and effective citizens. The course of study should expand rather than limit students' choices and opportunities. In such a school:

1. The curriculum clearly reflects the goals of the school, goals that emphasize the nature of the education the school seeks to provide. These goals are understood and accepted by staff, students, and parents and provide a vision of what the school is trying to accomplish.
2. A core of common learning is the essential component of the curriculum. This core comprises the majority of the school's graduation requirements.
3. The core curriculum provides for specialized programs and/or services for students with special needs, abilities and/or interests.
4. The curriculum is geared toward student outcomes, and student advancement through the curriculum and eventual graduation are based upon demonstrated proficiency.

5. There is a systematic attempt to collect information on student achievement and make adjustments to the curriculum on the basis of the results.
6. There is a constant effort to seek and consider new ways to achieve the school's goals more effectively.

Cocurricular and Extracurricular

The cocurricular and extracurricular programs of an excellent school are vital complements to the curricular programs. These programs:

1. directly reflect and enhance the goals of the school,
2. are characterized by high levels of student participation, and
3. result in a sense of community, common interest and ownership in the school.

IV. EXPECTATIONS

In an excellent school the following expectations are shared by all members of the school community:

Performance

1. Students are expected to invest their best efforts in their academic, cocurricular and extracurricular pursuits. Teachers accept no less.
2. Teachers present students with specific performance standards for each course or activity.
3. Teachers accept the responsibility to help all students achieve these performance standards.
4. Teachers communicate with parents when perfor-

mance falls below acceptable standards and offer recommendations and assistance for improvement.

Atmosphere

1. A strong, reasonable behavior code provides clear guidelines for student behavior.
2. The standards of the behavior code are communicated to staff, students and parents.
3. The behavior code is enforced consistently by the entire staff.
4. There is an effort to help students understand the rationale behind the provisions of the behavior code.
5. The relationships among all members of the school community are characterized by consideration and respect for others.

Recognition of Achievement

1. There is a constant effort to recognize and honor the achievements of the members of the Stevenson school community.
2. There is a constant effort to provide positive reinforcement to students of all ability levels.

V. RESOURCES

An excellent school has sufficient financial resources and facilities to support the academic, cocurricular and extracurricular programs of the school. We believe that in such a school:

1. There is a constant effort to attract and hold outstanding teachers and administrators.

2. Provisions are made to give staff members the opportunity to stay current in their fields.

3. The maintenance of the building and grounds reflects the pride in the school.

4. Physical facilities are adequate and appropriate; the facilities meet the needs of students and the educational programs of the school.

The format of the report that results from the statement-writing process is of no significant consequence, and the conclusions as to what makes up an excellent school may vary widely from district to district. The report of another district that completed this process is provided below as a second example of format.

An Excellent High School

I. Provides a sense of community

A. Goals are widely recognized and widely shared.
B. There is a sense of a common mission.
C. Members of the school demonstrate consideration and concern for the rights and feelings of others.
D. Teachers, administrators, parents, and students take pride in their association with the school. They feel a sense of ownership in it.

II. Encourages high expectations for all

A. Teachers believe students can master the objectives of their course and take the responsibility to see that this mastery occurs.
B. There is a sense of "academic press."

1. Students are encouraged to give their best effort at all times.

2. Instructional time is protected.
3. Scholarship is honored.

III. Maintains an orderly atmosphere that promotes self-discipline

  A. A few general rules provide a framework for expected behavior.
  B. Students gain more autonomy as they progress through the school.
  C. The rates of student suspensions, expulsions, and withdrawals are low.

IV. Emphasizes quality instruction

  A. There is frequent observation of instruction and useful feedback to teachers.
  B. There are frequent professional dialogues regarding instruction.
  C. There is ongoing monitoring of student achievement.

V. Values teachers

  A. There is support for and recognition of good teaching.
  B. Teachers are given autonomy in determining instructional strategies.
  C. Teachers are encouraged to pursue professional growth.

VI. Encourages participation in the total school program

  A. Students engage in a variety of cocurricular activities.

B. Students support activities in which they are not actively involved.

C. Teachers demonstrate interest in student activities.

VII. Is never satisfied

A. There is a systematic analysis and evaluation of the factors mentioned here.

B. There is acknowledgment of those areas in which there is a discrepancy between goals and practice.

C. There is a continuous effort to improve.

STRATEGIES FOR DEVELOPING A STATEMENT OF EXCELLENCE

Excellent organizations are characterized by a sense of vision. There is a common understanding about where the organization is headed and about what is valued. Schools are no exception. If schools are to move toward excellence, they must first develop a sense of what they want to become. We believe an important first step in creating this shared sense of vision is reaching a consensus about a statement of excellence.

Reaching a consensus on a statement that describes an excellent school has many benefits. Not only does the time and effort spent in this endeavor have practical benefits as improvement plans are developed, but the process of working together and discussing issues helps create a sense of commitment, ownership, and unity of purpose.

The process of developing a consensus statement is begun by the principal, whose responsibilities are as follows:

1. Study of organizational behavior, change, development, and leadership. Particular emphasis should be given to understanding the research on effective schools and on organizational leadership.
2. Identify key individuals to be invited to serve on the committee that will oversee the effort to draft a statement of excellence. Selection should take into account representation of the diverse groups within the school district, the influence of the individual within his or her group, and the ability of the person to take a broad view when considering the ramifications of school improvement efforts. A key policymaker in the district should also be included on the committee.
3. Convene an initial meeting of the committee at which the group becomes acquainted with the consensus process for decision making, agrees on a statement of purpose, and becomes familiar with the research on effective schools and their practices.

The responsibilities of the committee are as follows:

1. Establish a process to engage different segments of the school community—teachers, parents, students, administrators, residents, etc.—in discussing what they would like their school to be. The committee should develop both an outline of and a timeline for this process.
2. Record the results of these different discussions and attempt to identify common characteristics cited by different groups.
3. Write a tentative composite description based on these common characteristics.

4. Ask each group to review and react to the composite description.
5. Write a revised composite description based on feedback from the different groups.
6. Seek approval for the revised composite description of an excellent school from each group. Repeat this step and the preceding one if necessary.
7. Present the final description to the board of education for consideration, adoption, and dissemination.

The final description of an excellent school will be the framework for building an excellent school. This statement of excellence provides the basis for developing the key values and guiding principles of the school.

CHAPTER TWO

Shared Values: The Essence Of Excellence

> . . . it is clear that organizations have, in fact, gained great strength from shared values—with emphasis on the "shared." If employees know what their company stands for, if they know what standards to uphold, then they are much more likely to make decisions that support those standards. They are also more likely to feel as if they are an important part of the organization. They are motivated because life in the company has meaning for them.
>
> Terry E. Deal and Allan A. Kennedy (1982,22) *Corporate Cultures*

The extent to which a vision or statement of excellence affects a school depends in large part on the degree to which that vision is reflected in the core values chosen as the benchmark for decision making. These values play a crucial role in determining the fundamental character of an organization. Thus developing, shaping and enhancing values is a critical step in the pursuit of excellence. Without a sense of shared values, staff members are left floundering.

Warren Bennis and Burt Nanus (1985) emphasized the importance of explicit, widely held organizational

34

values in their study of effective leaders. They found that such values provide a context of meaning to the members of an organization, helping them to know how they are expected to behave. An understanding of these values enables the members of the organization to make decisions without frequent appeals to higher levels because they know what results are required. Thus organizational values can both direct and empower the individual members of the organization.

In *Corporate Cultures*, Terry Deal and Allan Kennedy (1982, 22) observed, "In our work and study we have found that successful companies place a great deal of emphasis on values. In general these companies share three characteristics:

- They stand for something, that is, they have a clear and explicit philosophy about how they aim to conduct their business.

- Management pays a great deal of attention to shaping and fine tuning these values to conform to the economic and business environment of the company and to communicating them to the organization.

- These values are known and shared by all the people who work for the company, from the lowliest production worker right through to the rank of senior management."

Paraphrasing Deal and Kennedy, we can ascribe to excellent schools these three characteristics:

- They stand for something, that is, they have a clear and explicit philosophy or vision, a shared sense of purpose, and a common view of what makes for excellent schooling.

- The leaders of the district and individual schools pay a great deal of attention to shaping and fine tuning a shared set of values that reflect and promote the vision of an excellent school, and to communicating these values throughout the school district.

- These values are known and shared by all of those who work in the schools, from support personnel right through to the superintendent and board of education.

Peters and Waterman (1982, 280) also place great emphasis on the important role that values play in excellent organizations. "Every excellent company we studied is clear on what it stands for, and takes the process of value shaping seriously. In fact, we wonder whether it is possible to be an excellent company without clarity on values and without having the right sort of values." If a school or school district is to become an excellent organization, the day-to-day behavior within the organization must be guided by values that are themselves representative of the vision of excellence of the school or school district.

What are some core values that best reflect a commitment to excellence? In examining the dominant beliefs of the companies they describe in *In Search of Excellence*, Peters and Waterman (1982, 285) found these few basic values were consistently present in excellent organizations:

1. belief in the best

2. belief in the importance of the details of execution, the nuts and bolts of doing the job well
3. belief in the importance of people as individuals
4. belief in superior quality and service
5. belief that most members of the organization should be innovators, and its corollary, the willingness to support failure
6. a belief in the importance of informality to enhance communication
7. explicit belief in and recognition of the importance of economic growth and profits.

The last of these values clearly is not pertinent to schools. However, if one substituted "explicit belief in and recognition of the importance of student academic achievement" for the last value, these values could easily be applied to a school.

TRANSLATING VISION INTO VALUES

One school dealt with the task of identifying the values it held dear by creating a task force. After the school community described the ideal it was striving to achieve in its statement of excellence (as outlined in Chapter One), the task force extracted from this vision for the future a list of central values for teachers. The task force then presented these values to the entire faculty for consideration. After considerable discussion, the faculty endorsed the following statement of principles:

1. We will teach to the course objectives and provide evidence of student achievement of those objectives.

2. We will make full use of the instructional time allotted to us.
3. We will demonstrate our belief and expectation that all students can achieve the objectives of the courses to which they are assigned.
4. We will help to ensure an orderly atmosphere that is conducive to learning throughout the building.
5. We will treat all members of the school community with respect.

Several characteristics of this list are particularly noteworthy. First, it is brief. The longer the litany of "thou shalts," the less likely it is to be remembered by teachers and thus the less likely it is to be effective in guiding them. Second, it addresses the issue of student achievement and emphasizes that teachers must continually weigh their efforts in terms of impact on student achievement. Third, it gives direction to the daily decisions and activities of teachers. Each statement carries explicit expectations regarding the responsibilities of teachers. Finally, it provides for large measures of autonomy for the individual teacher. Although instruction must be directed to particular student outcomes, the teacher is left free to determine how he or she will see to it that students achieve those outcomes.

The list provided here is meant to serve as an example, not as a model. Each school should establish its own unique statement of values and should involve the entire faculty (and perhaps parents and students) in the process of establishing those values.

Once the values have been established, they must be institutionalized if they are to play an important role in the development of excellent schooling practices. Thus the question of how these values are institutionalized within the school is a critical one for school leaders. Although values are reflected in hundreds of small behaviors, many of them subconscious, we believe that there are three areas that must be addressed if a school is to reflect the values of excellence. These areas are planning, monitoring, and modeling.

PLANNING FOR EXCELLENCE

Developing detailed plans is an important aspect of translating values from word into action. It is vitally important that schools move beyond the discussion of excellence and develop specific improvement plans. If the talk about excellence is not translated into behavior, discouragement, pessimism, and cynicism will emerge. Developing specific plans for improvement is the first step in building trust. Plans are the leader's way of demonstrating a commitment to the values that are central to a culture of excellence.

There are many ways to develop school improvement plans. The following is one that is easily adaptable to virtually any school or school district. This approach has been utilized by a number of districts in their pursuit of excellence.

Step One: Where Are We Now?

The first step in developing school improvement plans is to assess the current state of the school or school district in relation to the list of values that has been developed. The assessment should focus on specific characteristics with the school's values serving as the benchmark against which the school is measured. For example, one district assessed its schools in terms of the following characteristics: a planned curriculum, high expectations for students and staff, an emphasis on monitoring student achievement, a safe and orderly atmosphere, strong instructional leadership, students' pride in the school, a sense of satisfaction and high morale on the part of teachers, and parental support. These categories represented values that were consistent with the school's vision of excellence and gave direction to its improvement efforts.

Generally speaking, methods of gathering data about the current state of a school or school district should be multifaceted. Depending on the time and resources available, data-gathering procedures may range from conducting fairly simple surveys of opinion to compiling a complex array of statistics. The following are some commonly used means of assessing school practices.

- Faculty and Parent Perception Surveys. There are many excellent instruments available for surveying the perceptions of faculty and parents. These survey instruments are generally developed around the findings of research on effective schools. One problem with these instruments, however, is that the survey items may not adequately reflect all of the characteristics of excellent schooling practices that a particular school has agreed upon. Therefore, the instruments need to be adapted to fit a particular school's set of values.

- Interviews. The data gathered from the faculty and parent surveys often reflect broad patterns of perception. Follow-up interviews should be conducted in order to get more specific, in-depth response. The interview questions should be developed after the data from the survey instruments have been analyzed and should be designed to solicit elaboration about specific areas of the school program. One midwestern school district coordinated the interview sessions with a parent/teacher association meeting. Letters sent to the parents beforehand explained the purpose of the interviews, told how long they would take, and gave a few sample questions. At the PTA meeting interviewers were available in various rooms throughout the school. This procedure worked for the particular district because it was well planned and there was an excellent communication between the school district and those being interviewed.

- Observations. It is helpful to send observers into schools periodically to get information that did not emerge from the surveys and interviews. Data recorded by observers can also be used to validate the survey and interview responses. The observations should be informal and naturalistic. Training of observers need not be extensive, since the observations are not research-oriented in the strictest sense. Observers should be given some guidance as to what should be observed, such as traffic flow between classes, classroom teaching, cafeteria services, or attendance at club meetings. Observers should take detailed notes, recording only what they see and hear and not their feelings about what they observe. Schools that are assessing themselves do not always utilize observational data. However, the information gained from observations of the school's day to day operation can complement the other data collected.

- Examples of Student Work. Another important source of information is student performance data. Information should certainly include data on student performance on criterion reference and standardized tests. It should not, however, be limited to test scores. The quality of students' work in such areas as art, industrial studies, music, and debate, which often cannot be determined from standardized tests, is important if an accurate portrait of the state of the school is to be developed.

There are many other methods of assessing "where we are" in regards to excellence in schooling. The methods used are not crucial; what matters is that data are gathered about the school as it exists before school improvement plans are developed. Information on the state of the school will provide the baseline for developing plans and measuring programs. The quality of plans and of the evaluation of future improvement efforts will depend to a great degree on the quality of data collection and analysis during this step of the planning process.

Step Two: Where Are We Going?

Once those involved in the school improvement effort have reached some common agreement about the school's values and assessed the current status of the school in relation to those values, it is time for the next step. Step two is to bridge the gap between "where we want to be" and "where we are" by setting improvement goals for each of the categories in the school's statement of values.

The development of widely understood and widely accepted goals is a critical step in the school improvement process. Healthy organizations are goal driven, and their goals reflect the central values of the organization. Goal development is one of the most visible ways to institutionalize the values of an organization. As Charles Garfield (1986, 271) noted in his book *Peak Performers: The New Heroes of American Business*, effective goals give clear directions and, at the same time, maintain a unity of purpose. They help keep people on target so that they fulfill their visions. As Garfield concluded, "Goals are dreams with deadlines."

A statement of goals for improvement should include (1) an outline of specific plans for closing the gap between the present condition of the school and its ideal future state, (2) a management calendar or timetable for implementation, and (3) priorities. It is important to recognize that not all of the gaps can be closed at once. Some gaps are wider and more complex than others and thus may cost more and take more time to bridge. Improvement plans should be multi-year plans that set priorities as to what is to be accomplished in year one, two, three, and so on. There seems to be widespread agreement that significant school improvement requires more that one or two years. The quick fix just isn't available. Thus setting priorities and *persistently* pursuing long range goals are crucial aspects of a school improvement effort.

It is important that school improvement plans be reasonable. One of the reasons people fail to maintain their own personal renewal efforts is the same reason many school improvement efforts fail—the plans are unrealistic from the start. Most effective change takes place in small increments over a long period of time.

Thus change agents must exercise what Hyman Rickover (1985, 43) described as "courageous patience." It is much better to have a long string of small successes that begin to build a culture of excellence than to have gigantic flops from which it is virtually impossible to recover. Developing plans that are reasonable requires (1) an accurate assessment of both the problems and the resources that are required to resolve them as well as (2) a clear understanding of both the characteristics of personnel and the resources likely to be available.

Improvement plans should help people to identify not only where the school is going, but also exactly how it will get there. To communicate this message effectively, plans need to be clear, concise, specific, and as simple as possible. Peters and Waterman (1982) observed that in order for an organization to work, plans must be understood by those who make things happen. Some people have the tendency to equate the quality of improvement plans with their complexity, but this tendency must be avoided at all cost!

Finally, plans should be made public and should be presented with a sense of optimism and enthusiasm. A public announcement of goals communicates commitment to school improvement efforts.

MONITORING

Monitoring is another important way in which the core values of any organization are emphasized. Leaders monitor what they value most, that is, they check on and keep track of things about which they care deeply. All too often school officials espouse certain ideals and beliefs but then pay attention to other things. Students and faculty learn what is truly valued in a school by observing what school leaders pay attention to.

In both *In Search of Excellence* and *A Passion for Excellence*, emphasis is given to the practice of "management by wandering around," or MBWA. The point of this process is to monitor what is going on, to stay in touch. Leaders ask questions, observe, interact. In short, they *communicate*. Such intense interest in what's happening communicates some important messages. First, when leaders monitor they are saying, "We care enough about these values that we're keeping track of how we are doing in relation to them." How often have teachers been asked to help develop plans or projects only to have them die later from lack of attention? Second, monitoring raises expectations. One of the questions most frequently asked of those of us who work with the effective schools research is "How do you raise the level of expectations within an organization?" Although the answer involves attention to a number of areas, one element essential to raising expectations is simply paying attention to the things you value the most.

Money and Time: Benchmarks for Values

One way to get a feel for the congruence between actual behavior and the stated values of a school or school district is to monitor the spending of money and time. Schools frequently profess to value children's development of a strong self-image, but monitoring of the curriculum guides and lesson plans often reveals little time allocated to affective objectives. A school might proclaim that it values having students highly involved in activities such as intramurals, yet a survey of the budget may reveal little or no money allocated for these types of activities. If you want to see what a school or school district really values, monitor where the money is spent and what kinds of things are given the largest chunks of time.

Monitoring is such an important aspect of creating a culture for excellence that it should not be left to chance. Effective schools plan for monitoring. That is, good school improvement plans include ways in which plans will be monitored as they are being implemented. Planning for monitoring in the day-to-day operation of the schools is one way to ensure that attention is paid to those values which best reflect a school's vision of excellence.

MODELING

Does the behavior of the school district leaders model the behavior they expect from others? Is their day-to-day behavior congruent with their professed values? These are critical questions in any effort to incorporate values within an organization. In *Leaders: The Strategies for Taking Charge*, Warren Bennis and Burt Nanus (1985,186) put it this way:

> The leader is responsible for the set of ethics or norms that govern the behavior of people in the organization. Leaders can establish a set of ethics in several ways. One is to demonstrate by their own behavior their commitment to a set of ethics that they are tying to institutionalize.

Philip Selznick (1957) observed that the essential problem of leadership is the identification of key values and creation of a social structure that embodies them. Modeling is the way leaders advertise their personal values, as well as the central values around which the organization operates. It is very difficult for faculty and students to take seriously verbal pronouncements about values. Although they may even agree that the values espoused are essential ingredients of an excellent school, they will be somewhat skeptical of the whole school improvement effort until they begin to see these values reflected in the day-to-day behavior of the leader.

Self-Renewal

Nowhere is modeling more important than in the area of individual self-renewal. Development of an organization that is healthy, vital, and growing depends on individual self-renewal. If we want self-renewal to permeate schools and school districts, we need educational leaders who have learned to manage their own personal self-renewal well enough that they can lead others.

What values must leaders model to communicate a commitment to self-renewal? Obviously they must value growth and development instead of maintaining the status quo. They must be open to new possibilities. They must be optimistic about the future. Above all, they must show their commitment to self-renewal by not leaving their own to chance. As John Gardner (1965,11) explained,

> Exploration of the full range of his potentialities is not something that the self renewing man leaves to the changes of life. It is something he pursues systematically, or at least

47

avidly, to the end of his day. He looks forward to an endless and unpredictable dialogue between his potentialities and the claims of life, not only the claims he encounters but the claims he invents. And by potentialities I mean not just skills, but the full range of his capacities for sensing, wondering, learning, understanding, loving and aspiring.

A number of school districts include in their administrator evaluation programs the expectation that administrators will set at least one personal renewal goal as part of their overall goal-setting plan. Self-renewal goals may be physical, attitudinal, or intellectual in nature. Of course, many administrators set goals in more than one area. The primary point to be emphasized is that it is virtually impossible to institutionalize values that reflect a growing, dynamic, healthy, and exciting vision for schools unless the school leaders plan for their own systematic personal self-renewal.

Heroes: Visible Models of Values

Another way to model values is through the choice of "heroes." Which teachers are viewed as heroes by the students, the administration, and the parents? Which students do school personnel recognize and promote as heroes—the football star, the academic scholarship winner, or the handicapped youngster who with quiet dignity overcomes the odds and does well in school? Just as our national heroes reflect our general culture, our schools' heroes reflect the values of our schools. The

48

careful selection and promotion of heroes is a powerful means of communicating the values that are of greatest importance to a leader.

Deal and Kennedy (1982) observed that some of the most successful companies in America believe so strongly in heroes that they regularly, and subtly, create them. School leaders should follow suit, making heroes of those whose behavior embodies the values of their school.

STRATEGIES FOR ESTABLISHING AND MAINTAINING VALUES

Leaders of truly outstanding schools and school districts take the necessary steps to make sure that the school's key values are reflected in the day-to-day operation of the school. They develop specific, simple school improvement plans with goals that reflect the school's vision of excellence. They monitor how well the important values are exemplified by those who represent the school. They model the behavior they expect of others and make heroes of those who personify these characteristics they profess to value.

For those who are committed to school improvement we offer the following suggestions:

1. Through group meetings, reach some consensus about the key values your school should reflect.
2. Highlight these values in the faculty manual.
3. Insist that administrators model the agreed upon values.
4. Insist that teachers remain within the parameters of

49

these agreed-upon values, but otherwise provide them with large measures of autonomy in their day-to-day tasks.

5. Develop specific goals and plans for school improvement.

6. Develop specific plans for monitoring the day-to-day implementation of school improvement plans.

7. Discuss with faculty the kinds of signals that are being transmitted through the behavior of the administration and faculty. Identify areas that could be improved.

8. Develop programs that encourage individual self-renewal.

9. Develop plans for recognizing and rewarding administrators, faculty, students, and parents who exemplify the dominant values of the school. (See Chapter Eight.)

CHAPTER THREE

The Principal
As Leader

> If a school is a vibrant, innovative, child-centered place; if it
> has a reputation for excellence in teaching; if students are
> performing to the best of their ability; one can almost always
> point to the principal's leadership as the key to success.

U.S. Senate Resolution 359, (1970)

> Managers do things right. Leaders do the right things.

Warren Bennis and Burt Nanus (1985, 21) *Leaders*

One of the most consistent findings of the research on
both excellent businesses and effective schools is the
importance of strong leadership. Warren Bennis and
Burt Nanus (1985, 20) argued that organizations cannot
be successful without effective leadership which they
describe as "the key factor in the ability of business to
translate its vision into reality." In his examination of a
number of different studies of outstanding businesses,
James Lewis (1985) found that strong leadership was
one of the most consistent indicators of business excellence. Even Tom Peters and Robert Waterman (1982,
81-82), who insisted that excellent companies achieve

51

their excellence through the extraordinary efforts of ordinary people, acknowledged that these companies "have been truly blessed with unusual leadership."

The research on effective schools focuses particularly on the leadership of the principal. After visiting schools across the country Jane Eisner (1979, 59) reported, "The key to a school's success is the 'principal principle': the notion that a strong administrator with vision and with ability to carry out his or her goals can make an enormous difference in a school." Keith Goldhammer and George Becker concluded that excellent schools are inevitably led by aggressive, professionally alert, dynamic principals determined to provide the kind of educational program they deem necessary. Ron Edmonds (1979, 22) argued that one of the most tangible and indispensable characteristics of effective schools is "strong administrative leadership without which the disparate elements of good schooling can neither be brought together nor be kept together." Even Stewart Purkey and Marshall Smith, (1983, 443) who described their orientation to the effective schools research as skeptical and admitted that they were "suspicious of the 'Great Principal' theroy," acknowledged that "it seems clear that leadership is necessary to initiate and maintain the improvement process . . . [and] the principal is uniquely positioned to fill this role."

What is the role of the principal? Some descriptions of that role characterize the principal as a frontline supervisor, whereas others portray the principal as a middle manager. Some authors describe the principalship in terms of its functions—school-community relations, staff personnel development, pupil personnel development, educational program development, and business and building management. Others describe the principalship in terms of the various publics with whom the principal must work—staff, students, parents, other administrators, and the general public. We believe that recent research findings on effective organizations, effective leaders, and effective schools call for a new definition of the principalship, one that recognizes the four major roles of the principal:

1. promoter and protector of values
2. empowerer of teachers
3. instructional leader
4. manager of climate

In short, the effective principal must be both a leader and a manager. As a leader the principal must promote and protect the values of the school, empower teachers, and monitor and evaluate instructional effectiveness. As a manager the principal must work to maintain a climate that is both productive and satisfying. This chapter will consider the principal as leader. Chapter Four will deal with the principal as manager of climate.

THE BASIC DILEMMA: STRONG PRINCIPAL OR AUTONOMOUS TEACHERS?

The research on both effective principals and effective schools cites the importance of principals who serve as strong instructional leaders and closely monitor student achievement. Various studies have described effective principals as forceful, dynamic, assertive, energetic and quick to assume the initiative. Good principals have a sense of commitment and direction for attaining their goals. They take charge and wish to make the school over in their own image. Blumberg and Greenfield (1980) concluded in their study of effective principals that it takes a unique person first to help give a school an image of what it can be and second to provide the drive, support and skills to make that image approximate reality. It is almost impossible to read this research without visualizing dynamic, assertive principals who roam their schools with a clear vision of what they want to achieve and determination to achieve it regardless of the obstacles.

The research on motivation, however, seems to offer a distinctly different message to school administrators. Fredrick Herzberg (1966) conducted seventeen different empirical studies of diverse work groups to determine which factors were effective in inspiring unusual commitment and effort on the part of employees. Herzberg found that although factors such as salary, security, working conditions, and interpersonal relations could lead to worker dissatisfaction, they were ineffective in motivating individuals above and beyond the call of duty. Employees were inspired to exceptional dedication only when they believed in the significance of their work and felt a sense of recognition, responsibility, achievement, and advancement as a result of their efforts. Herzberg concluded that these motivational factors were best promoted by job enrichment, a management strategy that requires supervisors to yield or at least share some of their decision-making authority and give greater autonomy and responsibility to employees.

More recent studies of high performing and innovative companies have yielded similar findings. "Employee motivation is a complex science," wrote Deal and Kennedy (1982, 57), "but its foundations rest on the simple recognition that we all need to feel important in some phase of our lives." They found that the outstanding companies recognize this fact and give their employees lots of autonomy. Managers in these companies place a much higher level of trust in their fellow employees and are much more willing to delegate responsibility than managers in less effective companies. Rosabeth Moss Kanter (1983, 142) agreed that outstanding companies arouse "the desire to act" by providing "the freedom to act." Peters and Waterman (1982) found that the best run companies are able to inspire extraordinary commitment by extending a large measure of autonomy to their individual employees. Workers who are given the freedom to determine some of their goals and the autonomy to develop strategies to achieve them outperform their more rigidly supervised counterparts again and again.

Thomas Sergiovani (1967) applied Herzberg's research model to teachers with strikingly similar results. In his survey of over 3,000 teachers, Sergiovani found that although the notion of advancement is not a factor in teacher job satisfaction, the feelings of achievement, recognition, and responsibility that go with increased autonomy in the classroom are the most significant factors in teacher satisfaction.

The message this body of research sends to educators is clear: Give teachers more freedom in what they teach and how they teach it, and both their morale and their performance will improve. This is, in fact, the basis of the recent recommendations for educational reform offered by the Carnegie Foundation's Forum on Education and the Economy (1986). In its report entitled *A Nation Prepared: Teachers for the 21st Century*, the Forum called for reforms that would empower teachers and transform schools from bureaucratic, hierarchical societies into collegial communities in which teachers are treated as professionals and assumed to have the expertise needed to decide how best to do their jobs.

The seemingly contradictory messages of the research on effective schools and the research on motivation has presented a dilemma for conscientious principals. The message from the effective schools research seems to be "Take charge! Be a leader not a manager! Push and pull and prod until your personal vision of the school becomes a reality." The research on motivation, however, offers very different advice: "Empower your teachers! Give them the freedom and autonomy that will enable them to fulfull their personal and professional needs." What's a principal to do? What style of leadership is best suited for a school interested in the quest for excellence?

Choosing One At The Expense Of The Other

Many school administrators attempt to resolve the dilemma by subscribing to one school of research and ignoring the other. The administration of a nationally recognized high school has made a serious effort to apply the research on effective schools and its emphasis on monitoring student achievement. Administrators have established elaborate curriculum guides for each course, complete with specific objectives and unit examinations that assess student mastery of each objective. All instructors teaching the same course are required to follow the same day-by-day course outline. These teachers also administer identical unit tests on the same day, according to a testing calendar established by the administration. The tests are scored and results recorded in the testing center of the school, and thus administrators are able to monitor student achievement course by course and teacher by teacher. It is difficult to conceive of a more thorough monitoring of student achievement.

But what impact does this system have on classroom teachers? They are robbed of their professionalism by the assembly line mentality that characterizes this approach to instruction. They have little say about what is taught and virtually no opportunity to make decisions in such critical areas as pacing, reteaching, or assessment. Decisions regarding the complex task of teaching are made by individuals far removed from the classroom. Theodore Sizer (1985, 71) has argued that "autonomy is the absolute condition of effective teaching." Yet in this school and in schools across the country teachers are denied that autonomy in the name of the research on effective schools.

Meanwhile, other administrators have responded to the findings of the research on motivation by opting for a hands-off policy toward their staffs as the best means of ensuring autonomy and, therefore, high teacher morale. One prominent midwestern school district provides an excellent example of this laissez-faire approach to administration. There is no district-level curriculum in the school system, and thus each teacher is allowed to determine the content of his or her courses. Members of the same department who are teaching the same course are under no obligation to coordinate their efforts; they can decide independently what they will include and emphasize in that course. Once a teacher is awarded tenure in the district, he or she is free from the demands of formal observation and evaluation. Teachers know that after they achieve tenure they will never again have their classrooms visited by an administrator for the purpose of assessing instruction. The only schoolwide monitoring of student achievement that takes place is analysis of the performance of each graduating class on the ACT exam.

The administrators in this district take pride in the fact that they have enacted policies that provide academic freedom for each teacher. Indeed, it is difficult to imagine a school in which teachers have more autonomy in the area of instruction. Although one might anticipate that job satisfaction and teacher morale would flourish in such an atmosphere, a conversation with a veteran member of the faculty revealed otherwise. "We are told that the administration is determined to safeguard academic freedom, but to many of us it just comes across as administrative indifference," he admitted. "It seems as if no one but me cares how much or how well the kids learn in my class. It has been years since I have had any feedback on my teaching. I think many of us feel neglected, ignored. I know I'd like some recognition for my efforts in the classroom, and no one in this school except my students is in a position to give me that recognition."

The Solution: Simultaneous Loose-Tight Properties

The solution to the strong principal versus autonomous teachers dilemma is for the principal to be both an inflexible, autocratic protector of values and an enthusiastic empowerer of teachers. This solution is described by Peters and Waterman (1982) in terms of the concept of "simultaneous loose-tight properties." An organization identifies a few central values that will give direction to the activities and decisions of all its members and then demands *rigid adherence* (tightness) to these few non-negotiable values on the part of its members. At the same time, however, it promotes and encourages individual innovation and autonomy (looseness) in day-to-day operations. This approach allows leaders of an organization to emphasize the importance of control and freedom at one and the same time. Deal and Kennedy (1982) also found that excellent organizations rely on philosophical values to maintain a balance between control and autonomy. On the one hand, these values let employees know how they are expected to act and serve as a mechanism for sanctioning or proscribing behavior. On the other hand, the values eliminate the need for excessive rules and regulations because they give employees a common sense of direction.

The concept of simultaneous loose-tight properties has much to offer school leaders. A school that can identify a few key philosophical values which give clear direction to the daily activities of its staff, is able to resolve the dilemma of strong leadership versus teacher autonomy. Principals need not choose between exerting forceful leadership and encouraging teacher autonomy. By using the concept of simultaneous loose-tight properties, principals can serve as both demanding protectors of school values and enthusiastic empowerers of teachers.

THE PRINCIPAL AS PROMOTER AND PROTECTOR OF VALUES

In Chapters One and Two we argued that schools seeking excellence should base their efforts on explicit, widely understood statements of vision and values. The articulation of vision and values, however, will not have a significant impact on schools unless their principals accept as one of their essential responsibilities the promotion and protection of those values. Principals must know what they want, communicate what they want, and maintain a consistent position.

Effective Leaders Know What They Want

In his Pulitzer Prize-winning study of leadership, James M. Burns (1978) advised that the first step a leader must take if he or she hopes to influence others is to clarify his or her own goals. It is impossible for an organization to remain focused on its vision and values unless its leaders are certain of what the vision and values entail. In short, leaders must know what they want to accomplish. Bennis and Nanus (1985, 28-29) put it this way: "Leaders are the most results oriented individuals in the world . . . . This fixation with and undeviating attention to outcome, some would call it an obsession, is only possible if one knows what he wants."

Such clarity of purpose is particularly important in public schools, which have been called on to cure every ill and solve every social problem. Too often state legislatures or boards of education send the message that everything is important. As a result, nothing is done well.

The current situation in Illinois serves as a perfect example of this problem. As part of the legislature's educational reform package, the state board of education developed and disseminated over 3,500 specific learning objectives that every student in the state is to master by the end of the tenth grade. The teaching of various other topics is mandated by separate legislation. Schools must teach forest management, protection of wildlife, and humane care of domestic animals. Every teacher in the state is required to teach kindness, justice, and moral courage. Schools are to conduct exercises to show the value of trees and birds, to commemorate the life and history of Leif Erickson and the principles and ideals he fostered, to commemorate the American Indians, and to teach the contribution of Casmir Pulaski to the American Revolution. Meanwhile, the legislature has asked school officials to take time from the school day to allow all students to participate in the election to determine the official state bird. The axiom, "To have more than two goals is to have no goals at all," suggests the frustration inherent in such a situation.

The establishment of clear, purposeful focus is one of the most urgent needs facing our schools. An organization cannot stick to the knitting unless it has a clear sense of its purpose and mission. A principal who provides the focus necessary to clarify a school's mission has elminiated a major barrier to excellence.

Effective Leaders Communicate What They Want

Vision and values can influence an organization and those within it only if the vision and values are communicated. In fact, Bennis and Nanus (1985) concluded that the mastery of communication is essential to effective leadership.

What are the keys to communication that attract and inspire? Peters and Waterman (1982, 83) discovered that one key is redundancy—a "boorish consistency over long periods of time in support of . . . one or two transcending values." Bennis and Nanus (1985) cited the effective use of metaphors and slogans. Their advice to anyone trying to institute change is to ask, "How clear is the metaphor?" Thus, unlike most school administrators, who begin each school year with an explanation of what is new in the way of procedures and policies, effective principals will emphasize what remains the same—the vision and values that direct the efforts of those within their schools.

Furthermore, effective principals will repeat that message at every opportunity, recognizing that, in the words of Peters and Waterman (1982, 83), "no opportunity is too small, no forum too insignificant, no audience too junior." The principal of one high school that has made academic achievement its primary emphasis has a knack for including the school's slogan, "Where Minds Matter Most," in both written and oral communication. The principal of an elementary school committed to Sizer's notion that autonomy is the key to effective teaching coined the slogan "Student Achievement Through Teacher Empowerment" to help teachers and parents understand that commitment. A leader of a school that calls on teachers and students to give their best effort to enabling the school to achieve excellence might adopt the slogan "Doing Our Best to Be the Best."

Effective Leaders Build Trust by Maintaining a Consistent Position

Principals can use every available opportunity and the most creative metaphors to articulate their schools' values and still be ineffective communicators if the stands they take on a day-to-day basis are not consistent with those values. Bennis and Nanus (1985, 43) described trust as "the lubricant that makes it possible for organizations to work" and contend that leaders can establish trust only by being "the epitome . . . of constancy, of reliability." Effective leaders are predictable. They establish positions that are consistent with organizational values, make those positions known, and remain relentlessly committed to them. In other words, they stay the course.

Bennis and Nanus's concept of "building trust through positioning" is an extension of the saying, "Actions speak louder than words." It is the actions of leaders, not their exhortations, that communicate most clearly. As we suggested earlier, there are certain observable behaviors that suggest what is truly important to a school principal. Any assessment of a principal's effectiveness in communicating values should include the following questions:

1. *What does the principal plan for?* Does the principal develop long-term plans that are consistent with the mission of the school and are designed to instill its values? Does he or she share those plans with the staff and help them see the relationship between the plans and the mission? Does his or her daily planning provide an opportunity to concentrate on the factors that are most critical in advancing the school toward its vision?

2. *What does the principal monitor?* In their study of effective business leadership, Tom Peters and Nancy Austin (1985) argued that simply paying attention to what is important is the most powerful means by which a leader can communicate to and influence others. Throughout their chapter on leadership, they repeated the message, "Attention is all there is."

That axiom is an important one for principals to note. A principal who devotes considerable time and effort to the continual assessment of a particular condition within a school sends the message that the condition is important. Conversely, inattention to monitoring a particular factor indicates that the factor is less than essential, regardless of how often its importance is verbalized.

Often the values a principal communicates through monitoring contradict his or her professed values. The principal in one elementary school began the year with a speech urging teachers to embrace the district goal of improving student achievement. As an aside he admonished teachers for their overuse of the school copier during the previous year and insisted that they reduce the number of copies made for classroom use. An elaborate system was established to monitor the extent to which individual teachers were using the copy machine. Each time they used the machine, teachers were required to record their name, the date, what was being copied, how many copies were being made, and a brief explanation of why the copies were necessary. Every week a secretary would type a report based on the information from the log and present it to the principal. He, in turn, would record the results by teacher, keeping a running tally of the copies made by each. When a teacher was deemed to have been extravagant with the copier, that teacher was called before the principal and asked to mend his or her ways. Meanwhile, assessment of student achievement remained what it had always been, administration of a single standardized test, the results of which were presented to teachers without comment. The teachers in this school felt that the principal was communicating quite clearly what was *really* important to him.

3. *What does the principal model?* Principals who truly believe that the presence of certain values is

critical to the success of their schools will attempt to model those values. A school that calls on teachers to be analytical regarding their own teaching efforts should have a principal who is both a thoughtful student of teaching and an analyst of his or her own leadership style. A school that asks teachers and students to be considerate of one another should have a principal who models consideration in his or her dealings with all members of the school community. A school that claims to value its teachers should have a principal who treats them as professionals. In short, effective principals will make a conscious effort to embody the values of the schools they lead.

4. *What does the principal reinforce through recognition and celebration?* One of the most critical and powerful means of communicating and reinforcing values is constant attention to celebrating their presence within the organization. The importance of recognition and celebration has been cited repeatedly in the literature on effective business practices. Deal and Kennedy (1982) concluded that the values of an organization must be celebrated if they are to survive.

We believe recognition is a key to building the culture of pride that is found in excellent schools. A principal communicates values by recognizing and reinforcing those who act in accordance with those values. As Kanter (1983) pointed out, this public attention is important not only for the individual who receives it, but also for others in the organization who see that the things they might contribute will be noticed, applauded and remembered.

Recognition must not be used indiscriminately, however. Brookover (1982, 84) observed that principals often recognize and praise teachers for factors unrelated to effective instruction—"for not bothering the principal or for doing other pleasant and desirable things, such as having an attractive room, being well dressed, or being the life of the Friday afternoon get together." Recognition simply for the sake of recognition serves no purpose in the effort to improve a school. Celebration of behaviors and attitudes that are unassociated with the values of the school will send messages that are at best confusing and at worst counterproductive. Celebration can be a powerful factor in promoting particular values within a school, but the principal must ensure that association between the celebration and the values is clear (Chapter Eight is devoted to specific suggestions for celebrating the sucesses of a school.)

5. *What behavior is the principal willing to confront?* Although excellent companies encourage and reward individual autonomy, they insist that core values be observed and are willing to confront those who disregard such values. Their advocacy of these values may be described as rigid, non-negotiable, inflexible, and fanatical. Firings are generally the result not of poor performance but of the violation of values.

If principals wish to communicate the importance of particular values, they must be willing to confront those who disregard these values. If a school claims to value an orderly atmosphere throughout the building, the principal must be willing to confront the unruly student, the teacher who ignores misbehavior, or the parent who seeks to justify it. If a school claims to value teaching directed to particular student outcomes, the principal must be willing to confront the teacher whose instruction does not address those outcomes. If a school claims to value the best effort of teachers and students, the principal must be willing to confront those who give less.

Confrontation is not synonymous with personal attack, hostile discussion, or threats. Peters and Austin (1985, 373) described it as follows:

> a form of counseling in which the alternatives and consequences are clear and close at hand . . . a face-to-face meeting where you bring an individual's attention to the consequences of unacceptable performance . . . . Confronting recognizes that a change is imperative.

Nevertheless, the word "confront" may seem jarring to principals who have traditionally been urged to promote a collegial, cooperative working relationship with their teachers. Furthermore, principals are people too and feel the basic human desire to have the approval and esteem of those with whom they work. Confrontation seems both anti-collegial and unlikely to result in the approval of the person who is challenged. But the principal who seeks to lead will place the values of the school above the desire for popularity. Bennis and Nanus described the ability to do without the constant approval and recognition of others as one of the keys to leadership. Burns (1978, 34) put it this way: "No matter how strong this yearning for unanimity . . . [leaders] must settle for far less than universal affection . . . . They must accept conflict. They must be willing and able to be unloved."

We are not suggesting that principals assume an adversarial relationship with their staffs. We do believe, however, that if the values of the school are to be communicated in a clear and unequivocal manner, principals must be willing to confront students, parents, or staff members when their conduct violates those values. As Peters and Austin (1985, 373) concluded, "Quite

simply, nothing reduces the manager's credibility faster
that the unwillingness to address an obvious problem."

THE PRINCIPAL AS EMPOWERER
OF TEACHERS

What is empowerment? Kanter (1983, 18) described it as
"the degree to which the opportunity to use power
effectively is granted or withheld from individuals."
Basically it is the opportunity to act on one's ideas. The
concept of empowering workers has been embraced by
outstanding companies, and we believe that principals
who desire excellence must recognize that empowering
teachers is one of their most important responsibilities.

In describing the essential characteristics of leadership, Bennis and Nanus (1985) gave particular emphasis
to the fact that effective leadership empowers its work
force. Kanter (1983, 18) concluded that the empowerment of the work force is "one major difference between
those companies which stagnate and those that inno-
vate." Naisbitt and Aburdene (1985) argued that empowerment of the work force is a key characteristic of
outstanding companies.

Almost without exception, the best-run companies
have shifted the concept of the employee from one who
carries out orders to one who takes responsibility and
initiative, monitors his or her own work, and uses
supervisors as facilitators and consultants. They have
realized that the people who know the most about any
job are those doing it. The role of supervisor has also
been redefined; instead of giving orders, the supervisor
develops human potential. Like the transformational

leader described by Burns (1978), the supervisor must seek to tap the full potential of staff members and satisfy their higher needs.

Unfortunately the concept of empowerment has generally not been embraced by school leaders. A recent survey ("Teachers", 1986) of over 8,500 teachers revealed that only 28 percent of them could be classified as empowered. More that 85 percent of the respondents believed that quality of instruction would improve if they were allowed to increase their involvement in curriculum decisions. Only three out of ten teachers reported being involved in textbook decisions, and 80 percent said they were never consulted about who gets hired in the school.

Many administrators are reluctant to delegate authority to others because they believe it weakens their own power base. In his study of outstanding business leaders, however, Charles Garfield (1986, 182) argued that this concern is ill-founded. Garfield found that although successful leaders enjoy exercising control and responsibility, they recognize that their own power is amplified by the presence of powerful, capable colleagues. Leaders who develop, reward, and recognize those around them are "simply allowing the human assets with which they work to appreciate in value." The more they empower, the more they can achieve and the more successful the whole enterprise can become.

If schools are to make teacher empowerment the basis of school improvement, as the Carnegie Foundation (1986) recommended, administrators must embrace Garfield's finding that "power given is power gained." School leaders must be willing to break from the bureaucratic, hierarchical structure that has characterized public schooling and find ways to empower their teachers.

They must develop the skills that Garfield concluded are essential to successful empowerment—delegating, stretching the abilities of others, and encouraging educated risk taking. Following are some specific ideas for increasing teacher involvement in various areas.

1. *Developing the curriculum.* Chapter Five discusses a process for establishing a focused, school-wide curriculum. For now, we'll simply suggest that the teachers who will be responsible for delivering a curriculum should play a major role in its development. All teachers of a given grade or subject should be called on to arrive at a consensus as to what student outcomes should be achieved in that grade or subject and then should be held accountable for achieving those outcomes.

2. *Assessing student achievement.* Teachers should play a key role in developing the strategies for monitoring schoolwide achievement. If locally developed tests are to be used, teachers should work collectively to develop them. If standardized achievement tests are to be used, teachers should help select the tests that best fit the school curriculum. If alternative assessment strategies are to be used (for example, if evaluation is to involve writing folders, portfolios, or rating scales), teachers should be primarily responsible for developing the specifics of those strategies.

3. *Selecting instructional materials.* It seems obvious that the teachers who will use particular textbooks, equipment, and materials should have the major voice in their selection. But, as Peters and Austin (1985) pointed out, the idea that decisions should be turned over to the people who must do the work is both disarmingly simple and seldom put into practice.

4. *Planning and presenting staff development programs.* In most schools, if teachers are involved in the

planning of the staff development program at all, their involvement is limited to a survey of their interest in potential topics. Too often administrators select both the staff development topic and those who will present the topic to a passive teaching staff. However, one innovative school system demonstrated the role teachers can play in staff development. The principal established certain parameters for the staff development program:

1. Several options or themes had to be offered.
2. Options had to be based on teacher interests.
3. Each option had to provide for ongoing training.
4. The training had to include an opportunity to learn, practice, and receive feedback on a new skill.
5. Faculty members who were not interested in any of the themes could propose their own individual or small group staff development plan.

A faculty steering committee was then invited to assume responsibility for the planning and delivery of the program. The committee polled the faculty several times to identify five themes that were of interest to a significant number of teachers. Faculty members who were recognized as having particular interest or expertise in these five areas were then invited to work in teams of two or three to develop the program in that area. These teams assumed full responsibility for all of the decisions regarding their programs. Each team had to decide how it would make colleagues aware of the objectives and activities of its program, what funding would be required and how it would be allocated, whether to use local or outside speakers and resources, what materials would be required, and how the effectiveness of the program would be evaluated. The principal provided each team with support, time for planning, an adequate budget, and encouragement.

There are several benefits to this approach to staff development. First, it gives individual teachers an opportunity to pursue particular topics or develop their own improvement programs. Second, since teachers have a better understanding of the interest and needs of their colleagues than do the administrators who typically plan staff development, the programs they develop are more likely to be relevant. Finally, by giving recognition and responsibility to individual teachers, the program provides a means of developing leadership potential among the faculty.

5. *Determining instructional styles and strategies.* Although a principal can and should establish parameters for classroom instruction (for example, teachers will teach to the specified student outcomes, will make full use of the instructional period and will ensure that all students are actively engaged in the lesson), those parameters should stop short of mandating particular teaching styles. Some teachers thrive on individualized instruction, others are proponents of cooperative learning in small groups, and still others are both more comfortable and more successful with large group instruction. Forcing a particular mode of instruction on teachers robs them of both their professionalism and the autonomy they need to be effective. Certainly teachers should be encouraged to expand their repertoire and attempt to develop new skills. Certainly principals should discourage teaching behaviors that are inconsistent with the findings of the research on effective teaching. However, it is the results of teaching that should concern principals, not the style. Day-to-day instructional decisions should remain with the teacher.

6. *Scheduling*. Scheduling is a bone of contention at virtually all levels of public schooling. Elementary school teachers grouse about who gets which students and about having students pulled out of their classrooms for special programs in art, music, reading and so on. High school teachers compare class sizes and number of prepartions and scrutinize who gets assigned to teach which course. Why shouldn't teachers be invited to make these decisions collectively? Not only would they better understand the difficulties inherent in scheduling, but their collective deliberations might result in workable ways of resolving some of those difficulties. They are certainly likely to feel better about a teaching schedule that they had a hand in fashioning than about one imposed on them.

7. *Hiring new staff*. Teachers should play a role in the interviewing and selection of colleagues, particularly if they will be called on to work closely with the new staff members. If teachers at a particular grade level or in a particular subject are expected to coordinate their efforts, they deserve an opportunity to participate in the process of selecting new team members.

8. *Montoring*. One of the most important factors in the success of any organization is its effectiveness in helping new members understand its culture, or more simply, how things are done. Teachers new to a school have always believed, and rightly so, that the best source of this type of information is other teachers. Nevertheless, the formal programs that administrators have developed to orient and acculturate new members of a faculty have consistently failed to utilize veteran teachers.

The mentoring program established by one high school offers a refreshing exception to this general rule.

Each new teacher is assigned a mentor, who is then responsible for teaching the new-comer "how we do things around here." The mentors provide instruction and advice in virtually all areas of the school's operation, from such mundane matters as how chalk is ordered to such substantive issues as how student achievement is assessed. Mentors introduce their new charges to the school's teacher evaluation program by observing them in the classroom and giving them feedback on their teaching performance. This peer coaching takes place prior to the initiation of formal evaluation procedures by the administration.

The mentor program has received rave reviews not only from the new teachers but also from the mentors themselves. Teachers who are invited to serve as mentors take pride in being selected. Even though mentors receive no extra stipend for their service and are required to attend a training program during part of their summer vacation, every teacher who has been invited to serve as a mentor has accepted the invitaton.

Using teams to empower teachers

One of the most effective ways to promote innovation and a sense of ownership is by forming small units or teams within the larger organization. Recognizing this fact, outstanding companies have made excellent use of small coalitions. As Kanter (1983, 241) observed, "Whether called 'task forces,' 'quality circles,' 'problem solving groups,' or 'shared responsibility teams' such vehicles for greater participation are an important part of an innovating company." Naisbitt and Aburdene (1985) cited the movement away from an authoritarian hierarchy to smaller teams where people manage themselves as one of the fundamental shifts occurring in industry. Deal and Kennedy (1982) predicted that the small team concept will characterize organizations of the future.

The organization and use of small teams is a particularly promising possibility for schools. The individual classroom teacher works in isolation. The traditional grouping of personnel by faculty or department obscures the accomplishments and blunts the entrepreneurial spirit of the individual teacher. The crafting of coalitions and building of teams can heighten teachers' sense of involvement, responsibility and power. Thus we support James Lewis's (1986) call for school districts to move their organizations toward the small-team structure.

Teams can be formed in a number of different ways. We offer just a few examples.

1. *By grade level or subject.* For example. all teachers of a grade in a building could assume responsibility for carrying out the empowerment activities enumetated above for that grade.
2. *By similar teaching assignment.* For example, all teachers of accelerated or remedial students could work to develop or coordinate expectations, materials, assignments, disciplinary consequences, methods of evaluation, and so on.
3. *Interdepartmentally.* For example, all teachers of freshman-level courses in the humanities could work to develop particular themes to be emphasized across departments.
4. *In school-wide task forces.* For example, small groups of teachers could be formed to consider a particular problem and develop recommendations for resolving it.

There are a number of advantages to using the small team concept:

- It gives individuals a greater sense of control and thus greater personal involvements.

- It accentuates peer group pressure which Deal and Kennedy (1982, 184) described as "the single, strongest motivating factor for individuals in this post-industrial era."

- It builds consensus.

- It allows for the development of the leadership potential of a large number of teachers.

Cautions About The Use Of Small Groups

Small groups can be over-utilized or utilized badly. In some instances over-eager administrators have attempted to demonstrate their endorsement of the participatory, small-group process by convening task forces to consider the most trivial of issues. Surveys of teachers have consistently revealed that although teachers want to be included in deciding substantive issues, they do not wish to be involved in every decision. In other cases administrators have failed to provide members with a clear purpose and well-defined parameters. The most common error, however, is to assign a group responsibilities but fail to provide its members with the authority to fulfill them.

How can these problems be avoided? "Participation," wrote Kanter (1983, 243), ". . . needs to be managed just as carefully as any other organization system." She suggested that group involvement is inappropriate in the following situations:

- when one person clearly has greater expertise on the subject than all others;

- when those affected by the decision acknowledge and accept that expertise;

- when there is an obviously correct answer;

- when someone has the topic as part of his or her regular job, and it was not his or her idea to form the group;

- when no one really cares all that much about the issue;

- when no development or learning important to others would be served by their involvement;

- when there is a need to act quickly, and

- when people work more happily and productively alone.

The factor most critical to the success of the small group process is the willingness of the principal to give the group both significant responsibilities and the *power* to fulfill them. If principals recognize their responsibilities to empower teachers, the small group process can be a significant force in the effort to improve schooling.

Empowering Champions

Effective principals will pay particular attention to the important task of identifying and empowering champions—the zealous advocates who are willing to become personally committed to the success of an idea. Conventional wisdom in educational administration has long held that principals should not proceed with change until they have the approval, or at least the acquiescence, of all those who will be affected. However, Peters and Waterman (1982) found that it was the presence of champions, "monomaniacs with a mission," that was the key to initiating and sustaining change within successful business organizations. The same is true in education. We believe that the eventual outcome of an innovation depends more on the advocacy of an eager champion than on the passive approval of an entire staff. In fact, principals should be hesitant to proceed with an idea until a champion has embraced it. Thus the recognition, encouragement, and nurturing of champions is a key factor in any effort to improve a school.

What Empowerment Is Not

It is important to remember that empowerment is *not* simply turning people loose and hoping for the best. Peters and Waterman (1982) found that the corporate advocates of empowering the work force were not laissez-faire leaders; they remained obsessed with outcome. In fact, Ren McPherson of Dana Corporation supports empowerment precisely because it eliminates excuses for failure to perform; people cannot blame failure on the decisions of others when they are free to decide how to complete a task. Thus the principal who sets out to empower his or her teachers must, at the same time, demand that the values of the school be observed and continually monitor the progress the school is making in realizing its vision.

The image of principal as both a relentless, autocratic protector of values and a transformational leader seeking new ways to empower teachers is somewhat paradoxical. However, Peters and Waterman (1982) concluded that the ability to conceptualize and manage this paradox is a key to successful leadership and organizations. Schools must be both loose and tight; principals must both encourage innovation and insist on compliance. As Rosabeth Moss Kanter (1983, 248) said; "Freedom is not the absence of structure, letting employees go off and do whatever they want, but rather a clear structure which enables people to work within established boundaries in a creative and autonomous way."

THE PRINCIPAL AS INSTRUCTIONAL LEADER

Studies of effective schools consistently cite the fact that such schools have principals who act as strong instructional leaders. In one of the earliest and most widely cited studies, George Weber (1971) listed strong instructional leadership from the principal as one of eight schoolwide characteristics that influenced student achievement. Studies by the New York Department of Education (1974), the Maryland State Department of Education (1978), Brookover and Lezotte (1979), and the California State Department of Education (1977) are among the many that have emphasized the critical importance of having a principal who acts as a strong instructional leader. Ron Edmonds (1979) found that one clear difference between improving and declining schools was that in the former principals acted as instructional leaders. Even those studies in which instructional leadership was identified as coming from a source other than the principal—a central office administrator or a group of teachers—acknowledged that the principal provided the cooperation and support that made the leadership of others possible. In their study for the Rand Corporation, Paul Berman and Milbrey McLaughlin (1975, 20) considered the support of principals so important to school improvement efforts that they described principals as "gatekeepers of change." James Lipham (1981, 15) went so far as to assert that "no change of substantial magnitude can occur in any school without their [principals'] understanding and support." It seems clear that much of the success of any school's effort to move toward excellence will depend on the instructional leadership of the principal.

But what does instructional leadership mean? What do principals do to demonstrate that they are instructional leaders? In its summary of the research on effective schools, the Northwest Regional Educational Laboratory (1984, 7-8) identified several behaviors that characterize instructional leadership:

- understanding the school's mission and stating it in direct, concrete terms in order to establish a focus and unify the staff;

- portraying learning as the most important reason for being in school;

- demonstrating the belief that all students can learn and that the school makes the difference between success and failure;

- establishing standards and guidelines that can be used to monitor the effect of the curriculum;

- protecting learning time from disruption and emphasizing the priority of efficient use of classroom time;

- maintaining a safe, orderly school environment;

- monitoring student progress by means of explicit performance data and sharing those data with the staff;

- establishing incentives and rewards to encourage excellence in student and teacher performance;

- allocating resources according to instructional priorities;

- establishing procedures to guide parental involvement;

- maintaining two-way communication with parents;

- expressing the expectation that instructional programs improve over time;

- involving staff and others in planning implementation strategies;

- monitoring the implementation of new practices and programs;

- celebrating the accomplishments of students, staff, and the school;

- knowing, legitimizing, and applying research on effective instruction;

- making frequent classroom visits to observe instruction; and

- focusing teacher supervision on instructional improvement.

Providing Instructional Leadership Through Teacher Supervision

It is impossible for principals to function as instructional leaders unless they are willing to monitor teaching by venturing into the arena where instruction takes place, the classroom. In addition, they must be sufficiently knowledgeable about effective teaching practices in order to provide teachers with meaningful feedback on their instructional strategies and methods.

Principals who do not choose to be instructional leaders often balk at the time commitment that is necessary to provide the kind of supervision that improves instruction, arguing that their managerial duties do not allow them to devote time to instructional improvement. Effective principals find the time. In his review of research on effective principals, Lipham (1981, 14) wrote, "Effective principals are skilled in time management and find opportunities to plan cooperatively with teachers, visit and observe classrooms, provide teachers with helpful feedback, and evaluate the progress of both staff and students." In order to make time to provide meaningful supervision, a principal may have to persuade the local board of education that teachers should be formally evaluated every two or three years rather than annually. Research on adult learners indicates that they need an opportunity to practice and to receive timely feedback when they are attempting to acquire a new skill; thus an evaluation program in which teachers receive feedback three or four times in one year and then are not formally evaluated the next is superior to one in which they are visited only once each year.

In addition to somehow managing to spend considerable time in the classroom, principals must, if they are to serve as instructional leaders, find time to develop the expertise necessary to assess the effectiveness of instruction. As Gordon Cawelti concluded, "The difference between effective principals and others seems to lie in their knowledge of quality instruction." We realize that many principals have neither sufficient knowledge of the research on effective teaching nor adequate observation and conferencing skills to help teachers improve their instruction. We contend, however, that if schools are to move toward excellence, principals must take responsibility for developing such knowledge and skills.

Charles Garfield (1986) found that the peak performers of the business world have a sustained commitment to personal and professional growth and development. They identify what skills they need to be successful and assume responsibility for developing these capabilities. Principals who hope to lead a school on the quest for excellence must emulate these peak performers. They must recognize that if they are to be the instructional leaders that effective schools require, they must become students of good teaching, improve their classroom observation skills, and develop effective conferencing techniques. Subsequent chapters will offer suggestions in each of these areas and will outline an instructional supervision process designed to enable a principal to serve as both an empowerer of teachers and a strong instructional leader.

STRATEGIES FOR ENHANCING THE LEADERSHIP OF THE PRINCIPAL AND THE EMPOWERMENT OF TEACHERS

Following are some strategies we recommend to principals interested in enhancing both their own leadership and the empowerment of teachers:

1. Play a key role in identifying and stating in writing the key values of the school.
2. Replace the rules and regulations in the faculty manual with the school's statement of values.
3. Initiate discussions of the school's statement of values with individual teachers. Can they articulate these values? If not, you have work to do.
4. Review your long-term and short-term goals. Does your planning reflect the values of the school?
5. Review your speeches and writings of the past six months. Have you referred to the values of the school?
6. Develop slogans and metaphors to communicate the values of the school.
7. Outline what and how you have monitored in the past six months. Do the time and attention you have devoted to monitoring communicate what you feel is truly important? Remember, attention is all there is.
8. Advise every member of the administrative team to give priority to the identification and recognition of students and staff who are advancing the values of the school.
9. Read Chapter Eight on celebrating success and implement three of the ideas suggested there. Better yet, establish a team to create a plan to celebrate achievement.

10. Develop or purchase an assessment instrument that gives teachers an opportunity to provide you with feedback on your performance. Compare your perceptions of what you are communicating and modeling with the perceptions of your staff.
11. Conduct that meeting you have been putting off with the staff member whose performance has slipped. Remember the advice of Peters and Waterman (1982) to be tough with values but tender with people.
12. Give teachers greater control of the curriculum. Let teams of teachers establish the scope and sequence of content areas, specific outcomes for each course, and methods of assessment. Monitor the results.
13. Identify individuals or small teams of teachers who have particular talents and interests and give them the authority to plan and present an ongoing staff development program.
14. Let teachers work collectively to develop their teaching schedules.
15. Involve teachers in the hiring of new staff members.
16. Use teams to problem solve, create new programs, and develop and deliver instructional programs. Start modestly and develop a record of success before expanding the team concept.
17. Encourage internal competition among individual teachers or teams of teachers by providing them with comparative data on their performance.
18. Work with the staff to develop a mentor program to assist in the orientation of new staff members.
19. Identify a champion and provide that person with the time, resources, and encouragement he or she needs to complete a project successfully.
20. Interview teachers individually to determine what's

working and what's in the way. Work with them to develop plans for removing the barriers to their effectiveness.

21. Arrange your schedule so that you can devote at least 25 percent of your time to observing classes and discussing instruction with teachers.
22. Read everything you can on effective teaching.
23. Develop expertise in the synergetic supervision process explained in Chapter Seven.

CHAPTER FOUR

The Principal As Manager Of Climate

The ambience of each school differs. These differences appear to have more to do with the quality of life and indeed the quality of education in schools than do the explicit curriculum and the methods of teaching.

John Goodlad (1985, 14) in *Pride and Promise: Schools of Excellence for all People*

A positive school climate is perhaps the single *most* important expression of educational leadership.

Scott Thompson (1970, V) Foreword to *Improving School Climate*

There is no mistaking the fact that schools have a certain "feel" to them. A study conducted for the Maryland State Department of Education (1978, 17) explained that an effective school "gives an immediate impression that it is 'being run' as opposed to 'running'. There is an air about the school that suggests it has a direction, a point of view, and an orientation." Even casual visitors can ascertain whether a particular school environment is threatening or friendly, idle or productive, repressive or relaxed. Edgar Kelley (1980) labeled this feel school climate, the prevailing or normative conditions that are relatively enduring over time and can be used to distinguish one environment from another. Wilbur Brookover (1979) defined school climate as the collective set of attitudes, beliefs, and behaviors within a building that make up the group norm.

Discussions of organizational climate often focus primarily on the degree of satisfaction expressed by the members of the organization. A school that seeks excellence, however, must be more than just a warm, friendly place. It must concern itself with achievement by establishing high expectations, challenging students and teachers, assessing performance, and holding individuals accountable. Therefore we prefer to regard climate as a measure of both the satisfaction of teachers and students *and* productivity which, in the case of a school, is described in terms of student achievement. Studies have shown the following characteristics to be in evidence in schools that have been found to be particularly effective with respect to student achievement:

- Teachers have high expectations for student achievement. They are confident of their ability to teach *all* students and accept their responsibility to do so.

- Instructional time is protected from distractions.

- The school atmosphere is orderly and generally conducive to learning.

- Learning progress is monitored closely.

Each of these characteristics conveys a sense of

academic press. Teachers and students recognize that academic achievement is both expected and valued. Instructional time is regarded as too important to waste. Behavior that interferes with a teacher's ability to teach or a student's ability to learn is not tolerated. Procedures are in place to assess student achievement, and the results are shared with students and faculty. In short, the norms, attitudes, and procedures at work in an effective school reinforce the notion that learning is the central mission of the school. There is an ecology of high expectations that affects teachers and students alike.

The research on effective schools has consistently pointed to the principal as the key figure in shaping the climate of a school. As the National Institute of Education (1978) concluded in its study of school violence, strong school governance on the part of the principal is the key factor in providing an orderly and productive educational environment. Brookover (1982) contended that the major responsibility for shaping climate rests squarely with the principal. Kelley (1980, 53) put it this way:

> If there is a single tool a principal should have, it is a mirror. Looking in that mirror, the principal can find the person who more than any other is both responsible for and accountable for the feelings of satisfaction and productivity for staff, students and patrons.

Given the tremendous influence of the principal on school climate, a basic issue confronting principals is how to exercise that influence in a positive way. We believe that the most effective principals monitor and manage climate in much the same way as do the excellent business executives described by Peters and Waterman (1982)—by making a conscious effort to keep in touch. If principals are to monitor and influence the climate of their schools, they must emulate the business executives who establish what Peters and Waterman (1982, 121-22) described as "a vast network of informal open communications . . . a virtual technology of keeping in touch." Here are some suggestions for establishing such a network.

MBWA

It is a tribute to the popularity of *In Search of Excellence* that the phrase "management by wandering about" (MBWA) has become something of a cliche. The idea behind MBWA is simple: Managers should escape from the confines of the office for a good part of each day to keep in almost constant informal contact with others in the organization. They should be highly visible and close to the action.

The idea of MBWA has its corollary in the research on effective schools, which frequently cites the high visibility of the principal as a characteristic of excellent schools. In fact, in light of the remarkable unanimity of opinion on the importance of MBWA, the infrequency with which it is put into practice is equally remarkable. Even the best-intentioned principals tend to become trapped in the office—bogged down in paper work and day-to-day concerns. Principals of schools committed to excellence must recognize that they cannot monitor the pulse of the school from the office or motivate by memorandum. Nor can they leave something as important as MBWA to chance. Principals schedule appointments, meetings, and classroom visits in their daily calendar, why not MBWA? They should block out a time on their calender each day for their MBWA sorties. The time should be varied so that they do not see the same people every day. Contacts should go beyond exchanging casual greetings to discussing significant issues, sharing information, commending achievement, inviting questions, and responding to rumors. We believe that schools will be well served if principals devote as much time as possible to MBWA each day.

Hold Daily Meetings of the Administrative Team

Meetings of building level administrators are traditionally held infrequently (weekly or monthly) and conducted according to a formal agenda. In large schools these meetings may be the only times administrators see each other. As a result, minor problems and concerns are often allowed to fester and accumulate, and the regularly scheduled meetings can deteriorate into gripe sessions.

One suburban high school resolved this problem by initiating brief, daily meetings of the administrative team. The principal and department heads meet over coffee each morning for twenty minutes. There is no formal agenda, and any member of the team can raise an issue for discussion. Topics can be continued over several consecutive mornings, but the twenty-minute deadline is always observed. The administrators in this school found that the practice of holding daily team meetings—a practice that is also observed by many of the nation's best-run companies—had many positive results. Minor problems and concerns could be resolved almost immediately. The lengthier, more formal weekly meetings became more productive, since they could be reserved for more substantive issues. Most important, the informal daily contact helped to build a sense of the administrators as a team united in purpose and effort. When the principal proposed the idea of daily team meetings, almost every department chairperson objected to the intrusion on his or her time. Today they agree that, as a result of the meetings, their administrative team is functioning more effectively than ever before.

The idea of frequent, informal meetings can also be used effectively in smaller elementary schools. An enterprising principal can establish a schedule of daily meetings to confer with teams of teachers—for example, Monday mornings, the first grade team; Monday afternoons, the second grade team; and so on. The key is not format or formality; the key is communication.

Teach

Peters and Waterman (1982) reported that the leaders of America's best-run companies make a concerted effort to stay close not only to employees but also to customers. Thus they periodically serve as salespeople for their companies' products, respond to customers' complaints, assist in production, and so on. These executives find that being close to the customer gives them valuable feedback and new insights. Furthermore, their participation in the primary tasks of the organization emphasizes the importance of those tasks.

This "close to the customer" policy is also advisable for principals. They must have empathy for the concerns of teachers and students, and there is simply no better way to become personally involved in the nitty-gritty of the teacher-student experience than by teaching.

There are several benefits that will accrue to a principal who returns to the classroom:

- *A closer relationship with students*. Particularly in large high schools, students view the principal as a distant and remote figure. He or she is a voice over the public address system, a face at infrequent assemblies, an occasional passerby in the hallway. A return to the classroom provides the principal with an opportunity to establish a deeper, richer relationship with at least a portion of his or her students. This makes the principal seem more approachable to all students.

- *Greater empathy for teachers*. Principals tend to forget the frustration of dealing with an unmotivated student, having instruction interrupted by a message from the attendance office, being obliged to carry out administrative tasks such as distributing passes, or facing the student who needs additional help because she has been on a family vacation for three weeks. Although a return to the classroom may not produce any remedies for teacher frustration, at least principals will develop a better understanding of faculty sentiment.

- *Greater credibility with teachers*. A return to the classroom endows a principal with greater credibility when he or she is evaluating the instruction of teachers. Faculty members who are looking for a reason to dispute or ignore the instructional recommendations of a principal have a tendency to fall back on comments like "It's been ten years since you were in the classroom; that idea won't work now." Furthermore, if the principal is really good in the classroom, models good teaching, and establishes a reputation as an excellent instructor, his or her recommendations for instructional improvement will carry considerably more weight than those of a principal who has not taught a class in a decade.

Practicing principals are almost certain to react to the suggestion that they teach with the response, "Where am I suppose to find the time?" The concern is a real one. Studies of the principalship reveal that the typical principal is already devoting nearly sixty hours to the job each week. We can counter that concern only by stressing the importance and benefits of a principal's staying in touch with his or her school through teaching. We agree with Theodore Sizer (1984) who insisted that any principal who doesn't have time for teaching should reassess his or her priorities.

One possible solution to the time crunch is to teach units rather that entire courses. In one high school, the principal teaches a three-week unit each quarter. During this time the regular teacher is released from the class to pursue a project of interest. The principal is responsible for all instructional tasks—developing lesson plans, finding materials, writing tests, sending failure notices etc.—and it is his job to assign each student a grade for the unit.

We recognize that keeping in touch with the climate of a school by such means as MBWA, daily meetings with an administrative and/or teaching team, and regular stints in the classroom will require considerable energy on the part of the principal. Nevertheless, like Peters and Waterman, we question the vitality of any organization whose leaders do not practice this peripatetic management style.

THE CRITICAL IMPORTANCE OF GOOD DISCIPLINE

According to Abraham Maslow's oft cited hierarchy of needs, people cannot attend to their higher needs until their baser needs have been satisfied. Thus a person's essential physiological needs must be met before he or she will consider higher needs such as security, belonging, esteem, and, ultimately, self-actualization. Applying this analogy to a school, we might say that the need for the safety and orderliness that accompany good discipline must be satisfied before the school can address higher needs such as a well-articulated curriculum, instructional effectiveness, teacher empowerment, and, ultimately, sustained educational excellence.

Of all the issues confronting public education in the United States, the issue of greatest concern to the American people has consistently been the lack of student discipline in the schools. For the past seventeen years the Gallup organization has conducted an annual poll to determine public opinion about the nation's schools. In every year but one, "lack of discipline" was regarded as the single biggest problem confronting the schools. Use of drugs, another issue associated with student behavior, was the second most frequently mentioned problem. Discipline and drugs combined elicited nearly four times as much concern as *any* other issue in Gallup's 1985 survey. A task force on school violence and discipline (1984, 10) appointed by President Reagan in 1984 concluded that "school disorder is among the most significant and perhaps the most overlooked, civil rights issue of the 1980's."

Obviously a school with a reputation for poor discipline will not be regarded as excellent by the community it serves. But public opinion and community perceptions are not the only reasons for a school to examine its practices in the area of student discipline. Virtually every study on effective schools has cited the ability to maintain an orderly atmosphere conducive to learning as a prerequisite to providing an effective school. As the presidential task force (1984, 11) concluded, "If the American education system is to achieve excellence, the problem of disorder in the schools must be addressed." A principal interested in leading a school to excellence simply cannot afford to overlook this critical area of school climate.

Common Pitfalls In School Discipline

A key element in the disciplinary program of any school is the effectiveness with which students are made aware of expectations regarding their behavior. All too often schools fail to communicate expectations. Some schools provide no guidelines at all, apparently expecting students to learn of the standards of appropriate behavior through some sort of osmosis. Other schools bury students in volumes of specific rules and regulations. Authorities in such schools attempt to anticipate every act to which they might object and then enact a rule forbidding it. However, students tend to be devilishly creative in inventing new situations that are not specifically forbidden by the list of do's and don'ts, and thus the rule book of a school that subscribes to this approach seems to be constantly expanding.

A second problem with the approach many schools take to student discipline is that there are no positive incentives for students to remain within the rules of the school. School disciplinary systems are generally built on disincentives or penalties for failure to observe the rules. If a student is willing to risk a short-term consequence such as detentions, a parent conference, or a suspension as the price for a certain activity (for example, cutting a class), the school offers no positive inducement to refrain from the activity. As a result, the student can reasonably conclude that his or her best interests are served by violating the rule.

A third problem with the disciplinary programs of many schools is the tendency to treat all students the same way. Schools have traditionally had difficulty in maintaining the appropriate balance between two important but seemingly contradictory goals. On the one hand, school officials seek a degree of control. They believe it is important to regulate both the conduct and the course of study of their students. On the other hand, educators realize the importance of teaching students to act responsibly, something that can be accomplished only when there is an element of choice. Throughout most of the history of public education, schools responded to this dilemma of control versus freedom of choice by emphasizing the former. All students were expected to follow a prescribed curriculum and observe the same rules and procedures. In the 1960s and early 1970s, the emphasis shifted to freedom of choice. Open classrooms in elementary schools and open campuses in high schools suddenly provided all students with the opportunity to determine how they would spend their time, and a proliferation of activities and courses enabled them to choose from a number of alternatives in each subject area.

The flaw in both approaches lies in that all students are treated the same way. Schools make no effort to discriminate between those who need structure and control and those who do not. Seniors who have exceeded every expectation of their high school and are only months away from the freedom and responsibility of colleges or careers are dealt with in exactly the same manner as entering freshmen.

Finally, administrators and faculty of some schools fail to acknowledge their responsibility to maintain an orderly atmosphere within their schools. In blaming the students, unsupportive parents, a permissive society, or the court system for student misbehavior, these educators have created a self-fulfilling prophesy that both ensures the continuation of inappropriate behavior and absolves them of the responsibility for correcting it.

A Positive Approach to School Discipline

The pitfalls cited above can be overcome if a principal is willing to:

- base the disciplinary code of the school on a few general guidelines or values,

- provide students who abide by those values with increasing privileges as they advance through school,

- insist that all staff members assume responsibility for the consistent enforcement of those values, and

- respond promptly and consistently to students who do not adhere to those values.

This positive yet assertive approach to school discipline can help to establish the orderly atmosphere that is a prerequisite for an excellent school.

Establishing Key Values to Direct Student Conduct

Chapter Three discussed the importance of providing teachers with a few key values to guide their daily activities. Providing students with such values is also important. Few of us can remember pages and pages of specific rules and regulations, but we can keep a few general guidelines in mind. If the disciplinary guidelines of a school are truly meant to be useful in directing the activities of students and teachers, if they are truly meant to become part of and to shape the culture of a school, a concise statement of general values is far superior to an encyclopedia of rules.

In one nationally recognized school, the principal led the faculty in a discussion of the general principles of conduct that all students should be expected to observe. The faculty identified two such principles: (1) student behavior should not infringe on the rights of other students, and (2) student behavior should not infringe on the teacher's ability to teach. Those principles now serve as the foundation for the entire disciplinary program of the school.

Another district used a task force of students, teachers, administrators, and parents to identify values that all students were to be encouraged to emulate. The task force decided to describe the conditions that would ensure a student's success in school. They came up with the following statement:

> We believe that students are likely to enjoy greater success in school and more satisfaction with their school experience if they:

- conduct themselves in a manner that contributes to an orderly atmosphere and ensures the rights of all individuals within the school;
- are considerate of others—teachers, staff, fellow students, visitors, etc.;
- become involved in the extracurricular program of the school, and
- give their best effort to their academic and extracurricular pursuits.

This idea of establishing a few general rules to guide student behavior can also be extended into the classroom. The faculty of one high school decided to develop consistent classroom rules that each teacher could agree to endorse and enforce. All teachers agreed that the following four rules could be applied to any class, and they made a commitment to enforce them.

- Arrive to class on time and be prepared for the work at hand.
- Remain attentive to the task at hand during the full period.
- Be considerate of the rights and feelings of others.
- Respond promptly to the directions of the teacher.

Of course, the development of statements of school values or general classroom rules will be strictly an academic exercise unless steps are taken to ensure that every student is familiar with their content. The statement of values should be the basis for student orientation at the beginning of each school year. In traditional student orientation programs, expectations for student behavior either are not addressed or are presented by the administration in the form of a long list of "thou shalt nots." The positive nature of statements of values and expectations can enable orientation to take on a decidedly different tone. In fact, the orientation of new students can be conducted by student leaders who offer the statements as helpful hints for success rather than as threats.

An even more effective means of ensuring that students are well versed in the school's expectations for behavior is to require students to pass a test demonstrating their knowledge of those expectations. One school requires each incoming student to pass an essay test on its statement of values and withholds privileges until the student is able to do so.

Finally, each teacher should review and emphasize the school's guidelines for student behavior with his or her classes. An entire faculty stressing consistent guidelines for behavior can have a powerful influence on shaping student conduct.

Providing Meaningful Incentives for Good Behavior

Innovative schools have successfully established disciplinary systems that provide students with meaningful incentives for observing the rules of the schools. One such system, particulary well-suited for secondary schools, provides a graduated series of privileges that students can earn only by meeting the academic and behavioral standards established by the school. The steps in this sequence of privileges are as follows:

Freshman Year

— No privileges

— Students are under the immediate supervision of a teacher every period of the day.

— Students must report to a quiet study hall during any period in which they are not scheduled for a class.

— Students have an abbreviated (twenty-five minute) lunch period.

— Students may not leave the campus at any time during the day.

Sophomore Year
First semester:

— No privileges (same as above)

Second semester:

— Students may be provided with an extended (fifty-minute lunch period).

Junior Year

— Students may be provided with an extended lunch period.

102

— Students may be allowed to leave campus during their lunch period if their parents request this privilege in writing.

— Students may be allowed to determine how they will use their "free" time (that is, those periods in which they are not assigned to a class). Options include using the library, auditing a class, lounging in the student commons or designated area of campus, visiting a teacher, having a snack in the cafeteria, etc. However, students may not leave the campus.

— Students may be allowed to drive to school.

Senior Year

— Students may be provided with an extended lunch period.

— They may be allowed to leave campus during their lunch.

— Students may be allowed to determine how they will use their free time. They are free to leave campus during those periods in which they are not assigned to a class.

— Students may be allowed to drive to school.

— Students may be allowed to determine their schedule of classes. Although they are required to select a minimum number of classes, they can determine the sequencing of their classes and free periods. All other students are assigned classes by the computer.

A key to this system of graduated privileges is that the

privileges are not assigned automatically but are reserved for those students who have met the criteria
established by the school. Such criteria might include a
minimum grade-point average, no unauthorized ab-
sences, and no disciplinary referrals for a given grading
period. Since this system is intended to provide incentives for good behavior, it should be structured so as to
continually offer students additional opportunities to
earn privileges. Thus students who fail to meet the
criteria for privileges at the end of one grading period
should not be denied the privileges forever, but should
have an opportunity to earn them if their grades,attend-
ance, and behavior during the next grading period meet
the standard. In other words, the school should not
consider a student's cumulative record in awarding privileges, since doing so would make it impossible for
students who struggled at the start of a year to ever earn
privileges. By giving students a new opportunity each
grading period, the school can continually provide both
positive incentives for students who are trying to improve and reinforcement for students who have met the
standards.

A second key to this system of graduated privileges is
the provision that any privilege may be withdrawn from
a student at any time if he or she no longer meets the
criteria for receiving privileges. The opportunity to have
an extended lunch period, free time, or open campus
should be contingent upon the students continuing to
meet the standards and expectations of the school. Thus
seniors whose grades, attendance, or behavior begin to
slip should find themselves back in a supervised study
hall with the underclassmen.

This program of awarding and withdrawing student
privileges benefits a school in two important ways. First,

it provides students with an incentive to observe the rules of the school. Students soon realize that it is in their best personal interest to earn good grades and avoid disciplinary problems. Second, the school is provided with its most effective deterrent to misbehavior. Principals in schools that have adopted this system have found that many students who were unaffected by traditional disciplinary measures were extremely concerned about the prospect of losing a much-valued privilege. Upperclassmen who were nonchalant about detention or suspension viewed even a short-term loss of privileges and banishment to a study hall of underclassmen as a humiliating experience to be avoided at all costs.

One of the assumptions underlying this approach to student discipline is the belief that schools should not treat all students the same way but should discriminate in the amount of freedom they permit students to exercise. The amount of freedom given should be based primarily on the individual student's behavior record. Since freshmen have had no opportunity to demonstrate responsible behavior and generally benefit from considerable structure during their introduction to high school, they should have little or no opportunity to exercise freedom of choice. However, wisdom and maturity are not exclusively a function of age, and the opportunity to assume more responsibility for one's time and decisions should not automatically be conferred on students as they advance through school. To paraphrase Barry Goldwater, the equal treatment of students is no virtue; discrimination in dealing with students is no vice. Every student should have the opportunity to earn whatever privileges the school provides, but only those who meet the school's standards should be awarded those privileges.

Assuming Responsibility for Maintaining Good Discipline

In his staff development manual entitled *Creating Effective Schools*, Wilbur Brookover (1982, 176) bemoaned the fact that many educators seem to believe that there is little that they can do to resolve the problem of a lack of student discipline in their schools. Brookover listed several "myths" these educators have used to explain why they cannot be expected to maintain an orderly atmosphere in their classrooms and schools:

- Children in general are uncontrollable because of the permissiveness of society.

- Parents are no longer supportive of the school.

- Parents cannot control their own children.

- The courts have tied the hands of the schools in terms of student discipline.

- Teacher training institutions do not prepare teachers to deal with the problem of student discipline.

- Certain students, such as low-achieving students, minority students, or students from a low socioeconomic background, cannot be expected to behave.

Such attitudes are indefensible given what we now know about effective schools and effective teachers. As Brookover (178) concluded, "Schools and teachers DO make a difference . . . . It is the behavior and techniques used by the school and teachers which are the primary determinants of the level of discipline." The presidential task force (1984, 20) concurred when it concluded that the reason schools had failed to come to grips with discipline problems was "the lack of 'will' of school officials to take action."

It should be obvious that attitudes and beliefs about discipline will play a major role in shaping the climate of a school. Certain attitudes must prevail if a school is to be excellent:

- The entire administration and faculty must believe in their ability to create the disciplinary climate of the school.

- The principal must make it clear that each staff member is to assume responsibility for maintaining discipline, not just in individual classrooms but throughout the entire school.

- Teachers must be familiar with the school's standards of student conduct and work to enforce those standards throughout the building.

- Students must be aware of the school's standards of conduct and, at least at the secondary level, believe that if they observe those standards they will be rewarded with increasing privileges.

- Students must recognize that violating the standards of conduct will result in disciplinary measures that are fair, firm, and, most important, inevitable.

Responding Promptly to Disciplinary Problems

The principal of an excellent school must work to instill the school's values in teachers and students by consistently enforcing the standards of conduct of the school. Student challenges to these standards are certain to occur. When they do, it is imperative that school officials neither ignore them nor overreact to them. Ignoring the violation of a rule suggests to students and teachers that the school's espousal of the importance of the rule is insincere; overreacting to a violation increases the likelihood that the student will see the response as a personal attack rather than the safeguarding of a standard of behavior.

The concept of logical consequences described by Rudolf Dreikurs and Loren Grey (1968) can be used to determine an effective response to the inappropriate behavior of a student. This concept calls for school officials to respond to a student who has violated a rule by (1) confronting the student immediately, (2) explaining the rationale for the rule, (3) reminding the student that in choosing to violate the rule he or she has also chosen the consequence that accompanies the misbehavior, (4) advising the student of the exact consequence that will occur should the student choose to violate the rule again, and (5) encouraging the student to stop the inappropriate behavior and observe the rules of the school. This approach to discipline enables school officials to focus on behavior rather than individual personalities and emphasizes to students that they are responsible for both their behavior and the consequences that result.

Ultimately, the success of this or any other approach to discipline depends on the prompt and consistent response of school officials to misbehavior. Principals must devote whatever energy is necessary to providing a response that is so thorough and consistent that students come to regard disciplinary action as the inevitable consequence of misbehavior. By so doing, they can establish a climate that Ron Edmonds (1979, 22) found was characteristic of effective schools—a climate that is "orderly without being rigid, quiet without being oppressive, and generally conducive to the instructional business at hand." Only when such a climate exists can a principal hope to turn the attention of teachers and students to the higher goals that lead to educational excellence.

STRATEGIES FOR MANAGING CLIMATE

Following are some strategies we recommend to principals interested in managing climate:

1. Review the daily schedule and weekly calendar. Identify intrusions on classroom time that can be eliminated. Ask teachers to help.
2. Unplug the public address system while classes are in session.
3. Review the distribution of the grades assigned by each teacher. Do any staff members have consistently high failure rates that suggest a failure to accept their responsibility to see to it that students learn? If so, it's time to confront the problem.
4. Schedule yourself for at *least* one hour of MBWA at a different time each day of the week.
5. Practice MBWA in such nonacademic settings, as athletic contests, lunch, dances, etc.
6. Hold brief, informal, no-agenda meetings each day with your administrative team and/or small teams of teachers.
7. Teach on a regular basis.
8. Identify the key values upon which you can build the school disciplinary code.

9. Require students to pass tests on the disciplinary code.
10. Turn a good share of your student orientation over to student leaders. Train them to articulate the values of the school.
11. Develop a series of sequential privileges that students can earn by observing the rules of the school. Remove privileges of students who fail to observe the rules.
12. Make certain that teachers are aware of and enforce the school's standards of conduct.
13. Use the logical consequences approach to discipline. Your response to misbehavior must be so consistent that students become convinced that misbehavior will inevitably result in a disciplinary consequence.
14. Keep parents informed of each disciplinary problem encountered by their children.

CHAPTER FIVE

Sticking To The Knitting: Developing A Focused Curriculum

Effective schools are places where principals, teachers, students, and parents agree on the goals, methods, and content of schooling. They are united in recognizing the importance of a coherent curriculum, public recognition for students who succeed, promoting a sense of school pride, and protecting school time for learning.

What Works (U.S. Dept. of Education, 1986, p.45)

The curriculum is the most important vehicle a school has for transmitting its core values to students. In fact, curriculum decisions represent the fundamental means of translating the value system of a school into the day-to-day experiences of both teachers and students. Hilda Taba (1962, p.68) put it this way:

Values are implicit in the very functioning of the culture, from the use of technical devices

111

to the requirements of job and civic participation. They are implicit also in institutional dynamics and the forms into which education is cast, from grouping to counseling. This means also that education for values is all pervasive and largely unconscious. The task of education is to make this process conscious, rationally defensible, and, as far as the role of the curriculum is concerned, more effective.

We believe that two critical issues must be considered when the curriculum of a school is assessed. The first is the fit—the congruence between the curriculum and the values of the school. Does the curriculum reflect the values that the school is attempting to promote? The second is the focus—the degree to which the curriculum identifies what is truly significant. Many schools suffer from curriculum overload; they attempt to do so many things that nothing is done well. Peters and Waterman (1982, p. 293) observed that effective organizations have a clear sense of what they are about and a focus that enables them to stick to the knitting. A school can stick to the knitting only if it has a clearly articulated curriculum that drives daily instruction.

THE CURRICULUM AND SCHOOL IMPROVEMENT: A RESEARCH BASE

As they begin the process of reviewing and improving the curriculum, school officials should familiarize themselves with existing research regarding the instructional program of schools. A review of the studies of effective schooling practices presents consistent findings regarding the importance of a well-planned curriculum that is monitored regularly. A synthesis of this research, compiled by the Northwest Regional Educational Laboratory (1984, pp. 7-11), is presented below. This research provides a helpful framework for school leaders as they begin their instructional improvement program.

1. The curriculum is based on clear goals and objectives.

   - Learning goals and objectives are clearly defined and displayed: teachers actively use building curriculum resources for instructional planning. District curriculum resources are used when available.

   - Clear relationships among learning goals, instructional activities and student assessments are established and written down.

   - Collaborative curriculum planning and decision making are typical. Special attention is focused on building good continuity across grade levels and courses; teachers know where they fit in the curriculum.

   - Staff, students and the community know the scope of the curriculum and the priorities within it.

2. Students are grouped to promote effective instruction.

   - In required subjects and courses, students are placed in heterogeneous groups; tracks are avoided; underplacement is avoided.

- Instructional aides and classroom grouping techniques are used to help keep the adult/student ratio low, especially during instruction aimed at priority objectives.

3. School time is used for learning.

- School events are scheduled to avoid disruption of learning time.

- Everyone understands time-use priorities; school communications highlight the need for time for learning; procedures are developed to maximize learning time.

- Time-use allocations are established among subjects taught; time-use guidelines are followed by staff.

- The school calendar is organized to provide maximum learning time. Prior to adoption, new instructional programs or school procedures are evaluated according to their potential impact on learning time.

- During the school day, unassigned time and time spent on noninstructional activities are minimal; the school day, classes and other activities start and end on time.

- Student pullouts from regular classes are minimized, either for academic or nonacademic purposes. The amount of pullout activity is monitored and corrective action taken as necessary to keep things in balance.

- Extra learning time is provided for students who

need or want it; students can get extra help outside of regular school hours.

4. Teachers and administrators continually strive to improve instructional effectiveness.

- Throughout the school there is an ongoing concern for improving instructional effectiveness. No one is complacent about student achievement; there is an expectation that educational programs will be changed so that they work better.

- School improvements are directed at clearly defined student achievement and/or social behavior problems; strong agreement is developed within the school concerning the purpose of improvement efforts.

- Priority goals for improvement are set which give focus to planning and implementation. Goals which specify desired changes in achievement or social behavior are known and supported in the school community.

- The full staff is involved in planning for implementation; specific recommendations and guidelines provide the detail needed for good implementation; plans fit the local school context and conditions.

- Implementation is checked carefully and frequently; progress is noted and publicized; activities are modified as necessary to make things work better. Everyone works together to help the improvement effort succeed; staff members discuss implementation and share ideas and approaches.

- Resources are set aside to support improvement activities.

- School improvement efforts are periodically reviewed; progress is noted and the improvement focus is renewed or redirected; successes and new goals are reported.

A SYSTEMATIC APPROACH TO PROGRAM DEVELOPMENT

Although the research on effective schools provides an important base for thinking about curriculum excellence, educators also need a framework for thinking about how to systematically develop curricular programs that have the fit and focus necessary to advance the core values of a school. The strategies and procedures for curriculum development that we offer here represent a general synthesis of several different approaches to curriculum development. These procedures, which can serve as a framework for developing either a schoolwide or a subject-specific curriculum, include the following:

1. developing a general philosophy that is consistent with the vision and values of the school,
2. developing goal statements, and
3. developing specific plans for the delivery of the curriculum.

Reaching a Consensus About Philosophy

If a school hopes to provide a curriculum that has the support of key groups within the school community, school officials must take steps to involve these groups in the curriculum development process. The strategies recommended in Chapters One and Two for promoting widespread involvement in the development of a vision and values are also well-suited to curriculum development. Teachers, parents, administrators, and representatives of the community should be involved in the earliest, most general discussions of the curriculum. As discussion begins to focus on particular content in individual classrooms, participation in the process should become more homogeneous with teachers playing the major role.

Initial discussions should consider basic philosophy. Just as a school benefits from a clearly defined statement of excellence regarding schooling in general, it also benefits from a widely understood statement of beliefs about what it plans to teach—the specific experiences it plans for students. This, quite simply, is the purpose of a statement of basic educational philosophy.

Many educators tend to dismiss educational philosophy as far too esoteric a subject to have any relevance to the daily concerns of their classrooms. Invite them to participate in a discussion of philosophy and you are quite likely to see their eyes glaze over. Discussions are much more likely to be productive if the issue is framed in terms of basic beliefs and assumptions. Almost anyone with an interest in education welcomes the opportunity to discuss ideas about such topics as the characteristics and needs of children, the expectations of the community for the school, the societal factors that should influence education, the relative importance of particular content or knowledge, and so on. Thus, the process of developing curriculum should begin with the following simple questions.

What Do We Believe About Students Who Will Be Attending Our Schools?

Discussion about the nature of the students should be both general and specific. In initial discussions participants should have the benefit of articles, pamphlets, speakers, films, or filmstrips that can help them to identify the general physical, intellectual, and emotional characteristics of the age group under consideration. Once members have that common background information, they can proceed to discuss their beliefs about the boys and girls who attend their particular school. The group should come to an understanding about the composition of the student body in terms of socioeconomic level; the percentage of students working below grade level, particularly in English and math; the percentage who go on to post-secondary education; the percentage enrolled in particular special education programs, and so on. The fundamental objective of these discussions is to develop a genuine and accurate feel for the nature of the students who are to be served by the curriculum the group is setting out to design.

What Are the Expectations of the Community for Our School?

Superintendents and principals can attest to the fact that schools do not operate in a vacuum; they must serve the public. Hence a curriculum development strategy should include an attempt to ascertain the desires and expectations of the community served by the school.

There are many ways to gather community input about what the school should be doing and what the curricular program should be emphasizing. Some schools have community meetings where the school program is discussed and community desires are made known. For example, a school district in the state of Washington hosts a goal-setting dinner each year. At this dinner, which is open to the public, an evaluation and analysis of the last school year is presented and a discussion is held concerning priorities for the coming year. Goals are discussed, clarified, and finally prioritized.

Involving a cross section of parents on school committees—especially curriculum committees—is another way to get community input. Some schools plan meetings in the homes of community members in various neighborhoods in order to attract parents who might not come to the school for meetings. This type of meeting is particularly effective for schools whose students are bused from many different neighborhoods. Refreshments can be served to add an informal touch. After refreshments, teachers and parents discuss the school and various aspects of the school program. In such an informal atmosphere people will often say things they would never have brought up in the more formal setting of the school.

Questionnaires, interviews, and telephone calls are still other ways to get input from the community. Whatever strategies are utilized, the important point to remember is that community acceptance and support are vital to the success of any school program. If community desires and expectations are ignored or even honestly misunderstood, serious problems are likely to develop in the day-to-day operation of the school.

What Are the Social Influences on the Curriculum?

Although it is important to consider what the local community expects of the school, those who have the responsibility of developing a school curriculum must remember that ultimately students will have to function in a larger society. If this fact is not kept in mind, schools run the risk of becoming narrow and provincial. Inattention to society and its trends increases the likelihood that schools will prepare students to operate in a world that simply will not exist. Study and discussion of contemporary life and of the larger society outside the school thus should be an important part of the goal-setting process.

Schools cannot teach everything. Increasingly, various interest groups are attempting to influence the makeup of the public school curriculum. Proponents of such programs as multicultural education, moral education, environmental education, drug education, and sex education are vying for space in the curriculum. Discussions about what the world will probably be like when the students leave high school can form the basis for deciding what to include in the curriculum and with what degree of emphasis. At the very least, a study of life in the larger society should play an important part in deciding what areas of the school program should be given priority.

What Are the Goals of Our Curriculum?

Discussions about the nature of the students, community expectations for the school, and contemporary society outside the school must ultimately yield written goal statements that are specific enough to give direction to the school program, yet general enough to allow consensus on the part of the various constituencies that make up the working groups. Writing these goals can be a rather difficult task, since different groups are likely to look at the school from very different perspectives.

120

As we suggested in Chapter One, it is often helpful to have one person write a draft of a position paper that seems to reflect the consensus reached in the working groups. This draft statement can then be duplicated and given to group members for their written comments. After the written comments have been discussed, the procedure is repeated until a document is produced that all members can endorse. The final statement may not be *exactly* what each person would want, but it should express beliefs and goals that each member of the group can support.

The final goal statements should be presented in the form of short, declarative sentences that are consistent with the statement of philosophy and give direction to the daily program. Normally these statements will be fairly broad and will encompass intellectual development, social and personal development, and physical development—in short, all areas of child growth and development. The statement of curriculum goals developed by the Memphis city schools after extensive community input is presented below as an example of district-wide goal statements.

RANK ORDER OF EDUCATIONAL GOALS FOR MEMPHIS CITY SCHOOLS

RANK	EDUCATIONAL GOALS
1	To develop a respect for property, the rights and ideas of others, and the ability to work well and cooperate.

121

2   To develop reading skills necessary for daily living.

3   To develop and maintain sound mental health through positive attitudes, curiosity for learning, and the development of individual abilities to the highest level.

4   To develop the skills necessary to depend on oneself for living with physical, mental, or emotional handicaps.

5   To develop and improve basic language skills with emphasis on the ability to communicate ideas and feelings effectively.

6   To develop the skills of a trade or improve present skills with opportunities for job counseling.

7   To develop an understanding of the importance of the school and community working together and the continuation of education in adult years.

8   To develop abilities in problem-solving and decision-making with an open mindedness toward many ideas and a willingness to explore alternative solutions to problems.

9   To develop an understanding of the effects of drugs, alcohol, and tobacco on the body.

10   To develop skills in basic mathematics and to develop the ability to apply these concepts to practical situations with emphasis on consumer math and management habits.

11   To develop independent and creative thinking for meaningful self-expression.

12	To develop understanding of the conditions needed for physical well-being.
13	To develop knowledge and appreciation of personal heritage, awareness of other cultures, and responsible citizenship.
14	To develop an understanding of man's relationship to his changing environment.
15	To develop appreciation for art, music, drama, and literature through opportunities for understanding and enjoyment.

Making the Philosophy and Goal Statements Public

Too often groups work diligently to develop philosophy and goal statements regarding the curriculum, only to see them filed away, never to be used again except for accreditation purposes. Philosophy and goal statements can be of enormous benefit to a school and its principal. First, these statements should be a primary consideration in determining the organization of the school. For example, should the school be organized along the traditional grade levels, or would interdisciplinary teams be more appropriate? Second, with interest groups increasingly trying to get their particular programs in the public school curriculum, written philosophy and goal statements can be helpful in establishing criteria for making decisions about adopting new programs. The principal who has a goal statement is in a position to say,

"Although I'm sure this is a very fine program, the faculty and parents at this school have decided that the school should place an emphasis on other goals." In other words, once goal statements have been agreed to, they can serve as the guidelines for future curricular decisions. Third, written goal statements provide a basis for program evaluation. Increasing pressures for accountability are making program evaluation more than something talked about in college classrooms and textbooks. A written philosophy and clear, concise goal statements that are reflective of that philosophy are prerequisites for an effective curriculum evaluation process.

How might one go about making the curriculum philosophy and goal statements public? A small, attractive brochure outlining the school curriculum can be produced inexpensively. The brochure should be made available to anyone, but especially to parents who will be sending their children to the school for the first time. The brochure should contain such information as makeup and size of the student body, data on the faculty, the philosophy and goals of the school program, a brief description of the curriculum, and other more mundane facts such as hours of school operation, telephone numbers, and processes to follow in case of an emergency.

Many schools have a framed copy of their curriculum philosophy and goals hanging in the lobby or somewhere near the entrance of the school. Such a display serves as a constant reminder of what the school is trying to accomplish.

Finally, the best way to make curriculum philosophy and goal statements public is to use them. Throughout the year groups and committees must be encouraged to make their curricular decisions in light of the school's philosophy and goals. By using the goal statements, faculty and students will heighten their awareness of what the school stands for and what is being emphasized in the curriculum.

PLANNING FOR LEARNING: DETERMINING AND SEQUENCING LEARNING EXPECTATIONS

The heart of curriculum development is the identification and sequencing of specific concepts to be taught. One approach to accomplishing this task is to have teachers meet together according to subject area. (Notice that as the curriculum development process proceeds, the involvement of participants becomes more specialized.) The first task facing each group is to reach a consensus about what concepts should be taught in each course in a particular subject area. Furthermore, the brainstorming techniques discussed earlier in Chapter one are once again useful at this stage of the process. The textbooks and workbooks that the students will be using are an important resource in these discussions.

For example, to determine the concepts to be taught in a middle school math program for grades 6 to 8, a group could first determine the last two concepts taught in the fifth grade of each feeder school. A math teacher from each feeder school could be asked to meet with the middle school math department, or it might be more expedient for a member of the middle school math department to visit each feeder school. Whatever procedure is chosen should then be repeated with the high school teachers in order to identify the first two math concepts taught in the ninth grade. When this task has been completed, the group has identified the first two concepts and last two concepts to be taught in the middle school math program.

The next step is to determine which concepts fall in between the previously identified concepts. One approach is to have a person at the chalkboard write down the concepts that individuals in the groups identify. The ideas should simply be listed rather than evaluated at this stage. After all ideas have been listed, they can be discussed in terms of appropriateness, possible combinations, overlaps and so forth. After a period of time, a consensus generally develops about which concepts students should be expected to master in each subject area. Agreement must then be reached on the sequence in which the concepts should be taught. Although this step is more critical in highly sequential subjects such as mathematics, it should be addressed in each subject area.

During this process each subject area group should rely on as many resources as possible. It is important to look at a number of different texts to see which concepts are included and the order in which they are presented. Teachers may wish to invite professors or teachers from other schools to offer suggestions.

The final listing of concepts to be included in each course should be general enough to leave teachers with some flexibility. Although it is critical to ensure that a common core curriculum is provided to all students, that curriculum should not be so crammed or tight as to require lock-step instruction that robs teachers of autonomy. Teachers must have some room to operate within the structure of the curriculum.

The final step in providing a curriculum that gives focus to daily instruction is to ensure that individual teachers incorporate the identified concepts into their unit plans. We offer two suggestions in this area. First, a unit plan should be written for each *major* concept that is to be taught in each subject area. Second, teams of teachers should write their own unit plans. Generally speaking, teachers seldom use unit plans or guides that have been developed by someone else. Furthermore, teachers are far less likely to feel a sense of ownership in materials if they had no part in preparing them.

An appropriate format for the development of these unit plans is one that requires teachers to answer the following four questions about each unit of instruction.

1. *What do I want the students to be able to do as a result of this unit?* To answer this question, teachers should simply list the behaviors that are expected of a student who has successfully completed the unit. This question requires an answer specific enough to force teachers to think in terms of outcomes, but not so specific as to require unreasonable work on the part of the teachers. (Notice that throughout this section educational jargon, such as "behavioral objectives," is kept to a minimum. Using clear, common-sense terms in the unit plan format will help communicate to teachers that unit planning is a practical endeavor that will be useful to them).

2. *How will I determine if the students are ready for this unit?* How will the teacher preassess students to determine whether they have the prerequisite skills and/or knowledge to be successful in the unit? Is it possible that students have already mastered the concept, in which case further instruction would constitute an inefficient use of time? Preassessment is an important component of planning and presenting instruction at the appropriate level of difficulty.

ing instruction at the appropriate level of difficulty. Preassessment may take many forms, such as a written test, a review of student homework, an evaluation of the test results from the previous unit, teacher observation of the students, or question and answer sessions. Whatever method is utilized, teachers should be able to indicate how they will know the students are ready for this particular unit. Thus this step requires teachers to identify the prerequisite skills for each unit of instruction.

3. *What methods and materials will I use to teach the lesson?* Teachers should have a clear idea of the methods and materials they plan to utilize in each unit of instruction. The constant modification and adjustment of plans based on student performance, which is the essence of good teaching, presupposes the existence of a basic blueprint of how the unit will be taught. One important consideration in preparing the unit plan is providing the opportunity for student practice. Although teachers should certainly be encouraged to include a variety of instructional methods in their unit plans, every unit plan should provide students with an opportunity to practice the behaviors they will be expected to perform as a result of that particular unit.

4. *How will I know whether the students have learned to do the things I wanted them to be able to do as a result of this unit?* There are a number of ways teachers might check to see whether the students have mastered the behaviors listed in the first step of each unit plan. Observation, written tests, questioning, review of homework, and examination of student projects are all appropriate means of making judgments regarding student progress.

Unit plans need not be lengthy—perhaps a page or two. A copy of unit plans should be on file with the principal or department chairperson, and periodically the unit plans should be put together in a curriculum guide for each subject area. Most important, each teacher should keep a copy of his or her unit plans and utilize it regularly.

A CASE IN POINT

The public schools of Jackson, Mississippi, have been widely recognized for their accomplishments in school improvement. Although the accomplishments of Jackson's schools cover a broad array of schooling practices, their most notable gains have been in the area of student achievement.

The superintendent of schools, Robert Fortenberry, is often asked, "Where did you begin?" "If we want to raise student achievement in our district, what should we make our first priority?" Dr. Fortenberry's answer: "The curriculum." Jackson's public schools spent one school year developing what they call their "common body of knowledge"—the list of skills and behaviors students are expected to master in each subject area. A booklet outlining these skills is available to parents and students as well as teachers.

The school district has also put a great deal of emphasis on developing a testing program that is in line with the curriculum. Although teachers are encouraged to teach more than they test, it is expected that teachers will *not* test what has not been taught.

In short, the tremendous gains in student achievement scores are attributable in large part to an increased focus in the curriculum and the development

FULFILLING THE PROMISE OF EDUCATION

of a testing program that is congruent with the instructional program.

STRATEGIES FOR IMPROVING CURRICULUM FIT AND FOCUS

Given that the central purpose of schools is to be a place where students learn, what they learn and how well they learn is something that cannot be left to chance. The curriculum should be consistent with, or fit, the vision and values of the school. Furthermore, schools should use the curriculum to establish a focus that enables them to stick to the knitting. Following are some strategies we recommend to school leaders interested in assessing the fit and focus of the curriculum of their school.

1. Review with faculty the findings of research on the curricula of effective schools.
2. Evaluate the curriculum. Is it consistent with the vision and values of the school? Does it help teachers and students focus on the most significant goals of the school?
3. Involve appropriate groups in developing specific curriculum improvement plans, making sure that the plans are consistent with the broader plans for general school improvement.
4. Charge teams of teachers with developing curriculum guides for each subject. For each major topic the guides should include a unit plan detailing intended student outcomes, strategies for determining whether students have the prerequisite skills and

knowledge, suggested teaching methods and materials, and strategies for assessing whether or not students have achieved the desired outcome.
5. Develop a systematic plan for assessing the effectiveness of the curriculum. (See Chapter Seven.)

CHAPTER SIX:

Excellence In Teaching

Even trained and experienced teachers vary widely in how they organize the classroom and present instruction. Specifically, they differ in several respects: the expectation and achievement objectives they hold for themselves, their classes, and individual students; how they select and design academic tasks; and how actively they instruct and communicate with students about academic tasks. Those who do these things successfully produce significantly more achievement than those who do not, but doing them successfully demands a blend of knowledge, energy, motivation, and communication and decision-making skills that many teachers, let alone adults, do not possess.

Jere Brophy and Thomas L. Good *Handbook of Research on Teaching* (1986, p. 370)

Central to excellent schooling is excellent teaching. It is obviously impossible to have an excellent school unless the instructional program of the school is characterized by excellence in teaching. To familiarize themselves with what is known about effective teaching, principals and teachers should become students of teaching.

TEACHING EFFECTIVENESS:
A THREE-DIMENSIONAL MODEL

Since teaching is a very complex act, any model of good teaching runs the risk of oversimplification. We favor a three-dimensional model which recognizes that the effectiveness of instruction is the result of the interplay among the teacher's knowledge, technical skills in delivering instruction (planning, pacing, clarity, questioning), and interpersonal qualities (enthusiasm, warmth, sensitivity, sense of humor). This three-dimensional model of effective instruction, adopted from Barbender and Eaker (1986), is illustrated below. Incorporated in this model is the assumption that improvement in any one area will increase overall effectiveness.

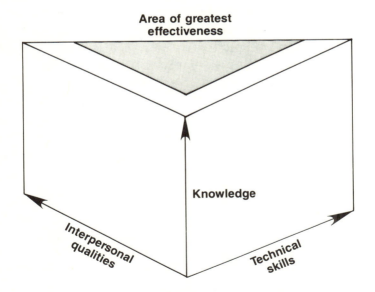

Three-Dimensional Model of Teaching

KNOWLEDGE

The essence of teaching is the transmission of knowledge to students. Thus one way in which teachers can improve their effectiveness is by improving their knowledge of the subject matter.

Efforts to improve instruction have generally been guided by the assumption that teachers have sufficient content expertise and thus require assistance only in the area of instructional process or delivery. Our observations, however, have indicated that some teachers present more current and accurate content that others. Occasionally a teacher will present information that is incomplete or just plain incorrect. Excellent teachers continually check their course content including instructional resources such as films, books, and handouts to ensure that it is accurate, relevant, and current. They read, take classes and attend workshops, and talk with other teachers. A school can be excellent only if it encourages such self-renewal on the part of teachers and promotes professionalism regarding subject matter content.

Organizing teachers into small teams is an excellent means of promoting continued learning. As teachers work together to plan, deliver, and assess instruction, they have an opportunity to evaluate the content of their lessons. The peer pressure associated with teaming is an excellent incentive to ensure both adequacy and accuracy of content.

TECHNICAL SKILLS FOR TEACHING

The majority of findings regarding teaching effectiveness focus on the technical skills of teaching—what effective teachers do when they teach. These findings, however, are not generic in the sense that they apply to each and every situation in the same way. The findings must be viewed in the context of specific classes, within particular subject areas and with specific students. In their review of the teacher effectiveness research, Jere Brophy and Tom Good cautioned, (1986, p. 370.)

> . . . this research also shows that complex instructional problems cannot be solved with simple prescriptions. . . . What constitutes effective instruction (even if attention is restricted to achievement as the sole outcome of interest) varies with context. What appears to be just the right amount of demandingness (or structuring of content, or praise, etc.) for one class might be too much for a second class and not enough for a third class. Even within the same class, what constitutes effective instruction will vary according to subject matter, group size, and the specific instructional objectives being pursued.

If those who seek to utilize the research on effective teaching keep this caution in mind, they will find that the research findings provide a useful framework for analyzing personal teaching behaviors and developing instructional improvement efforts.

The many studies dealing with instruction present a consistent picture of effective classroom practices. The synthesis of effective teaching research prepared by the Northwest Regional Educational Laboratory lists the classroom characteristics and practices that are associated with improvements in student performance:

Instruction is guided by a preplanned curriculum.

- Learning goals and objectives are developed and prioritized according to district and building guidelines, selected or approved by teachers, sequenced to facilitate student learning, and organized or grouped into units or lessons.

- Unit or lesson objectives are set in a timeline so that the calendar can be used for instructional planning.

- Instructional resources and teaching activities are identified, matched to objectives and student developmental levels, and recorded in lesson plans. Alternative resources and activities are identified, especially for priority objectives.

- Resources and teaching activities are reviewed for content and appropriateness and are modified according to experience to increase their effectiveness in helping students learn.

Students are carefully oriented to lessons.

- Teachers help students get ready to learn. They explain lesson objectives in simple, everyday language and refer to them throughout lessons to maintain focus.

- Objectives may be posted or handed out to help students keep a sense of direction. Teachers check to see that objectives are understood.

- The relationship of a current lesson to previous study is described. Students are reminded of key concepts or skills previously covered.

- Students are challenged to learn, particularly at the start of difficult lessons. Students know in advance what's expected and are ready to learn.

Instruction is clear and focused.

- Lesson activities are previewed; clear written and verbal directions are given; key points and instructions are repeated; student understanding is checked.

- Presentations, such as lectures or demonstrations, are designed to communicate clearly to students; digressions are avoided.

- Students have plenty of opportunity for guided and independent practice with new concepts and skills.

- To check understanding, teachers ask clear questions and make sure all students have a chance to respond.

- Teachers select problems and other academic tasks that are well matched to lesson content so student success rate is high. Seatwork assignments also provide variety and challenge.

- Homework is assigned that students can complete successfully. It is typically in small increments and provides additional practice with content covered in class; work is checked and students are given quick feedback.

- Parents help keep students involved in learning. Teachers let parents know that homework is important and give them tips on how to help students keep working.

Learning progress is monitored closely.

- Teachers frequently monitor student learning, both formally and informally.

- Teachers require that students be accountable for their academic work.

- Classroom assessments of student performance match learning objectives. Teachers know and use test development techniques to prepare valid, reliable assessment instruments.

- Routine assessment procedures make checking student progress easier. Students hear results quickly; reports to students are simple and clear to help them understand and correct errors; reports are tied to learning objectives.

- Teachers use assessment results not only to evaluate students but also for instructional diagnosis and to find out if teaching methods are working.

- Grading scales and mastery standards are set high to promote excellence.

- Teachers encourage parents to keep track of student progress, too.

When students don't understand, they are retaught.

- New material is introduced as quickly as possible at the beginning of the year or course, with a minimum review or reteaching of previous content. Key prerequisite concepts and skills are reviewed thoroughly but quickly.

- Teachers reteach priority lesson content until students show they've learned it.

- Regular, focused reviews of key concepts and skills are used throughout the year to check on and strengthen student retention.

Class time is used for learning.

- Teachers follow a system of priorities for using class time and allocate time for each subject or lesson. They concentrate on using class time for learning and spend very little time on nonlearning activities.

- Teachers set and maintain a brisk pace for instruction that remains consistent with thorough learning. New objectives are introduced as quickly as possible; clear start and stop cues help pace lessons according to specific time targets.

- Students are encouraged to pace themselves. If they don't finish during class, they work on lessons before or after school, during lunch or at other times so they keep up with what's going on in class.

There are smooth, efficient classroom routines.

- Class starts quickly and purposefully; teachers have assignments or activities ready for students when they arrive. Materials and supplies are ready, too.

- Students are required to bring the materials they need to class each day; they use assigned storage space.

- Administrative matters are handled with quick, efficient routines that keep class disruptions to a minimum.
- There are smooth, rapid transitions between activities throughout the day or class.

Instructional groups formed in the classroom fit instructional needs.

- When introducing new concepts and skills, whole-group instruction, actively led by the teacher is preferable.
- Smaller groups are formed within the classroom as needed to make sure all students learn thoroughly. Students are placed according to individual achievement levels; underplacement is avoided.
- Teachers review and adjust groups often, moving students when achievement levels change.

Standards for classroom behavior are explicit.

- Teachers let students know that there are high standards for behavior in the classroom.
- Classroom behavior standards are written, taught, and reviewed from the beginning of the year or the start of new courses.
- Rules, discipline procedures, and consequences are planned in advance. Standards are consistent with or identical to the building code of conduct.
- Consistent, equitable discipline is applied for all

students. Procedures are carried out quickly and are clearly linked to students' inappropriate behavior.

- Teachers stop disruptions quickly, taking care to avoid disrupting the whole class.

- In disciplinary action, the teacher focuses on the inappropriate behavior, not on the student's personality.

The preceding list of findings should not be translated into a checklist for the evaluation of teachers. The research findings do not constitute a recipe for improving instruction. Taken together they can, however, provide a broad base for analyzing teaching and creating an awareness among teachers of instructional behaviors that increase the probability of student successes.

INTERPERSONAL SKILLS OF TEACHING

Excellent teaching involves more than training students to score well on standardized tests. If we are to have the kind of schools in which teachers are viewed by parents and students as excellent, interpersonal aspects of teaching must be addressed.

The research findings regarding the interpersonal skills required for effective teaching are not nearly as strong and consistent as those regarding the more technical aspects of teaching. Nevertheless, an examination of the research on classroom and school climate, effective communication, and personality development reveals a fairly consistent picture of key interpersonal behaviors. Although the following ideas are not as well grounded in research as we would like them to be, we believe they can be useful as a starting point for discussions with teachers about the interpersonal aspects of excellence in teaching.

Quality of Communication

When we think of improving communication, we tend to think in terms of increasing the *quantity* of exchanges. However, with both individuals and organizations, it is the *quality* of communication that is most in need of improvement. This usually involves being a better listener, or as Carl Rogers put it, listening at all levels. If teachers are to be excellent communicators, they must do more that simply transmit subject matter effectively. They must communicate in such a way that students and parents will feel that they have been listened to—that the teacher really cares about them and what they are saying.

Empathy

There is a saying that excellent teachers remember what it was like to be a student. Helping students become successful is an important aspect of teaching, and it requires a willingness on the part of the teacher to see the student's side. There is a great deal that can be said about the importance of the teacher's ability to understand and empathize with students, parents, and administrators. Empathy does not imply excusing misbehavior; it merely implies realizing the world of the individual student, parent, or principal may be extraordinarily complex.

Respect

In the thousands of classroom observations that we have conducted, we have observed enormous variation among teachers in the amount of respect they give to and receive from students. It is important for teachers to

142

model manners and decorum when interacting with students. The difference between the climate created by the teacher who shouts at students to "shut up" and the one created by the teacher who responds to students with consideration and respect is apparent to both an outside observer and to the students in the class. Harshness should never be mistaken for firmness. Teachers can be firm and have high expectations for behavior yet still model respect for students.

Sensitivity

We were recently speaking with the mother of a child who was starting kindergarten. It was the first week of school, and the mother was explaining how nervous and afraid her daughter was about going to school. She pointed out that on the first two days of school the teacher was too busy taking care of other matters to greet the children as they arrived and make them feel wanted and welcome. Although being busy at times is unavoidable, it is important that teachers avoid becoming so busy that they forget the need to be sensitive to the feelings of anxious students.

Excellent teachers demonstrate their sensitivity in many ways. They are careful not only about what they say, but also about how they say it. They are careful about public criticism, and they do not tease or ridicule students. In short, excellent teachers demonstrate a sensitivity that communicates a sense of understanding and compassion.

Concreteness

Teachers can improve their interpersonal effectiveness by being aware that students need teachers to be specific and concrete. Often teachers encourage students to "do better." Rather than give such abstract directions, teachers should be specific about what students need to do in order to help themselves. Providing frequent, written concrete guidelines for improvement can be very helpful. They communicate to the student that the teacher has thought carefully about this individual student and what he or she needs to do in order to improve.

Genuineness and Self-Disclosure

Teachers can't "fake it" when it comes to interpersonal relations with students. Students generally know when teachers are genuine in what they say and do. Genuineness is related, at least in part, to self-disclosure by the teacher. Students are interested in their teachers. They want to know about them and what they are like. This doesn't mean that teachers should tell students everything about their personal lives. It merely suggests that students quickly get a feel for the genuineness of a teacher, and this feeling is affected by how much the students get to know the teacher as a person.

Concern

Do teachers care enough about students to confront them when they are harming themselves through their behavior? A black student in a primarily white high school remarked to the assistant principal, "Some teachers don't care enough about us to correct us!" Teachers should correct students if they throw paper down in the halls, if they do work that does not represent the best they are capable of doing, if they use incorrect grammar, and so on. This is one of the most powerful ways of saying, "I care about you and what happens to you."

Immediacy of Relationship

It is important for teachers to deal with students in the present—today, this week. All too often teachers dwell on the past history of a student in order to explain his or her inadequacies. Teachers also have a tendency to deal too much in the future: "Stay in school and get a good job!" We believe excellent teachers have a way of dealing with the students they are assigned in the present. They have an attitude that reflects the notion "I can't change the past or control the future, but what I can do is teach the students who are in my class today!"

Enthusiasm

Enthusiasm is contagious. Students mirror the enthusiasm of the teacher. It is virtually impossible to get students excited about learning, about discovering new things, and about seeing things in different ways if the teacher does not model enthusiasm. Enthusiasm is modeled in many different ways, ranging from moving around the room and utilizing a variety of teaching strategies to interacting with students and building on student ideas. Enthusiasm is more than any one thing teachers do. It is the combination of hundreds of individual behaviors that collectively communicates an attitude of excitement about what the teacher is doing. We believe enthusiasm is central to developing the positive interpersonal skills needed for excellence in teaching.

Warmth and Humor

Teachers in excellent schools are warm, caring people. It is difficult, if not impossible, to have an excellent school when teachers are cold, aloof, and indifferent to students.

In addition, teachers in excellent schools have a sense

of humor. We are not referring here to the ability to tell jokes. We're talking about the ability to see humor in situations and laugh at oneself. Schools are organizations that deal with people—the majority of whom are youngsters. This fact alone means that the very best plans are going to go awry from time to time. If teachers do not have a sense of humor, they will be miserable. They will not enjoy the students or teaching and will make life miserable not only for themselves but also for those around them. We think humor is an important ingredient in creating a positive climate.

Many educators are reluctant to include interpersonal qualities in discussions of effective teaching. There is neither a solid research base nor widespread agreement as to the specific behaviors that constitute positive interpersonal qualities. The relative importance of a particular interpersonal quality such as warmth is much harder to pin down than is that of a technical aspect of teaching such as questioning. Furthermore, it is much more difficult to effect change in personal behavior than in either knowledge or specific teaching strategies. Teachers can improve their knowledge of subject matter relatively quickly and easily by reading, attending workshops, and interacting with colleagues. These means can also be used to improve the technical skills of teaching if the element of practice is added. Improving interpersonal skills is a much more amorphous process and is usually accomplished only in small increments over an extended period of time.

We firmly believe, however, that any view of excellent teaching must include the interpersonal element. There is a tendency among researchers to measure that which is easiest to measure, but the fact that something is difficult to measure does not negate its importance or sug-

146

gest that it should be ignored. Teachers and administrators should discuss the interpersonal aspects of teaching and reach some consensus as to how this important area of teaching fits into the school's vision of excellence.

STRATEGIES FOR DEVELOPING EXCELLENCE IN TEACHING

If one accepts the premise that the excellence of a school is directly related to the quality of instruction that takes place in classrooms, it follows that principals and school leaders should become students of teaching. They should read about teaching, talk about teaching, think about teaching, and model an interest in teaching that will convey the message that quality teaching is central to the school's vision of excellence. Following are some strategies we recommend to school leaders interested in modeling this commitment to excellent teaching:

1. Hold workshops with teachers in which the research on teacher effectiveness is presented and discussed.
2. Hold seminars in which teachers can discuss specific aspects of teaching and share teaching techniques.
3. Acting on the belief that every teacher does something exceptionally well, have a teaching fair where teachers put on demonstrations and exhibits about specific activities or resources that work well for them.
4. Provide each teacher with a notebook containing research findings and ideas for effective teaching. Regularly give teachers new articles and research updates to read and add to their notebooks.

147

5. Encourage teachers to attend workshops, courses, and conferences that will improve their teaching skills.
6. Visit teachers' classrooms frequently so that classroom visits become a way of life in your school. Encourage teachers to visit and observe each other.
7. If possible, have teachers observe classes in other schools.
8. Make excellent teaching a major theme of the school's improvement plan.
9. Develop a teacher improvement/evaluation program that will encourage and help teachers to improve their instructional skills. (See Chapter Seven.)
10. Develop a process that will enable students to provide teachers with feedback regarding various aspects of teaching effectiveness, including the interpersonal aspects.

Monitoring:
Paying Attention
To What Is Valued

"Managing By Wandering Around: The Technology of the Obvious. It is being in touch with customers, suppliers, your people. It facilitates innovation, and makes possible the teaching of values to every member of an organization. Listening, facilitating, and teaching and reinforcing values. What is this except leadership? Thus MBWA is the technology of leadership. We will subsequently argue that leading (a school, a small business, or a Fortune 100 company) is primarily paying attention, and that the masters of the use of attention are also not only master users of symbols, of drama, but master storytellers and myth builders. All this can be accomplished only through means that are visible, tangible.

Tom Peters and Nancy Austin (1985, 31-32) *A Passion for Excellence*

Chapter Three stressed the idea that effective leaders monitor that which they value and believe is important. Monitoring, then, is a key vehicle for communicating the values of the organization. Although school leaders

149

should monitor all aspects of a school's programs, this chapter will focus on two areas in which we believe monitoring is critical to excellence: student achievement and teaching.

MONITORING STUDENT ACHIEVEMENT

Chapter Five discussed the importance of developing a curriculum that has widespread support, fits the vision and values of the school, and helps students and teachers to focus on the most significant areas of learning. The ultimate measure of the effectiveness of any curriculum, however, is student achievement. The research on effective schools consistently cites the monitoring of student achievement as a distinguishing characteristic of effective schools. We are convinced that the systematic collection and analysis of student achievement data should be a major component of any effort to create an excellent school.

In many school districts the effort to monitor student achievement begins and ends with the administration of a norm-referenced or standardized achievement test. Some districts have abandoned even this limited measure of achievement because of charges that standardized tests are racially biased or are never perfectly matched to the curriculum of the school. Administration of standardized tests certainly should not be the only method of monitoring student achievement. Such tests do, however, provide important information, particularly at the elementary level, and should not be abandoned. If school officials have taken the trouble to analyze different standardized tests to find one that closely matches the curriculum of their school, the results can provide a useful way of comparing the school to national norms. As Ron Edmonds (1982, 14) observed, "Despite all the limitations of standardized tests, I would argue as forcefully as I can that they are, at this moment, the most realistic, accurate and equitable basis for portraying individual pupil progress."

The monitoring of student achievement must go beyond the administration of standardized tests, however. The basic purpose of standardized tests is to determine how a student compares to a norm group. A school committed to excellence must also concern itself with whether or not each student has mastered the specific knowledge or skills that the school has identified as objectives. Thus criterion-referenced tests, in which each item is referenced to a specific learning objective that the student is expected to master, should also be used to monitor student achievement.

The Effective Schools Report (1983) lists the following characteristics of an ideal testing program:

1. Tests are locally developed to ensure that students are tested on what they are actually taught.
2. Tests are nationally normed to ensure that the local definition of mastery is generally congruent with student achievement outside of the district.
3. Tests are curriculum based to emphasize the key concepts of the curriculum to students and teachers.
4. Tests are criterion referenced to provide an assessment of each student in relation to the objectives established by the school.
5. Some tests are standardized to provide a general assessment of the school as it compares to national norms on the content measured.

A CASE IN POINT

Stevenson High School in Lake County, Illinois, used the above guidelines to develop a testing program that the National Center for Exemplery Educational Programs has described as being on the cutting edge of current assessent practices. This small (1,700 students) high school district managed to create and implement an assessment program in which the tests are locally developed, curriculum based, criterion referenced, and, at least in part, nationally normed. The program includes the following aspects:

1. Standardized Testing A. *General Achievement Test.* A general, norm referenced achievement test is administered to all eighth and tenth graders. The school uses the test both to assist with decisions regarding placement of students in particular courses and to identify how the average performance of its students compares with that of students from around the nation. Since the same test is administered to the same students twice, the school can also use the test to assess student growth. B. *American College Testing (ACT) Exams.* Over 90 percent of the school's graduates take the ACT exam. The composite results are used to compare the preformance of Stevenson students with that of the national sample. It is important that analysis of this sort takes into account any disparity between the percentage of seniors in a particular school taking the test and the percentage of seniors in the nation taking the test. As the percentage of students in a class taking the test increases, the average score for the group tends to decrease. Stevenson also participates in a pro-

gram offered by Northwestern University, in which the performance of students from forty suburban Chicago high schools on each subtest of the ACT exam is compared. Incorporated into the comparison is a factor for the percentage of a particular class that took the exam.

2. *Criterion-Referenced Testing.* The heart of the Stevenson assessment program is its criterion-referenced testing. All teachers identify the specific outcomes that students should be able to achieve as a result of enrollement in the course, and students are provided with a written description of these outcomes. The teachers then develop required, comprehensive final examinations in which each item is referenced to one of the specific course outcomes. Teachers who are assigned to teach the same course coordinate their efforts so as to present identical statements of outcomes as well as identical final examinations. Incorporated within the final examinations are appropriate items culled from nationally normed examinations such as the National Assessment of Educational Progress. These anchor items give teachers an indication of how the performance of their students compares with that of a national sample.

MAKING EFFORTS TO MONITOR STUDENT ACHIEVEMENT RELEVANT TO TEACHERS

One flaw in the monitoring programs of many districts is the failure to share the results with teachers in any meaningful way. As a result, teachers tend to regard the efforts to monitor student achievement as an administrative function that has little relevance to them. Furthermore, the fact that they do not have the benefit of the results means that teachers continue to work in isolation, receiving little or no feedback on the effectiveness of their efforts.

The value of monitoring student achievement arises primarily from its impact on individual classroom teachers. One of the most significant aspects of the Stevenson High School program is that it provides individual teachers with external indicators of their effectiveness. Stevenson uses a computer program to do a thorough analysis of the results of all final examinations. Each examination is subdivided into as many as fifteen different subtests. Each teacher is then provided with a printout that shows how his or her students performed on each subtest and on the entire examination in comparison to all other students in the school who completed the exam. The teacher also receives a report on the performance of students who took the test in previous years. Finally, a report on the nationally normed anchor items allows the teacher to see how his or her students performed in comparison to a national sample. Thus teachers are able to compare the performance of their students with that of the current students of their colleagues, past students, and students from around the nation. In short, they receive local, longitudinal, and national indicators of their teaching effectiveness.

What are the advantages of a system that requires such coordinated efforts on the part of teachers and provides them with such extensive feedback? We believe there are many.

1. The system ensures attention to a common curricu-

lum. If a school administration truly believes that all students should master certain outcomes, it should take steps to ensure that those outcomes are addressed, regardless of who teaches a particular course. Teachers should play the major role in developing both the student outcomes and the final examinations, and they should be given the freedom to decide how the outcomes will be addressed on a day-to-day basis. It should be made clear to teachers, however, that all students should have had an opportunity to achieve the outcomes by the end of the course. Common final examinations provide teachers with focus and serve as a check on their attention to the curriculum.

2. The system results in better tests. Tests written by a team of teachers are generally better than tests written by individuals because teachers critique one another's questions for relevance, clarity, congruity with outcomes, and so on.

3. The system promotes teamwork. Remember that the studies of excellent organizations consistently cite the beneficial effects of working together in small teams. Common examinations are a spur to teamwork among teachers of the same course or the same grade level.

4. The system motivates teachers. Studies of excellent organizations have concluded that the peer pressure arising from working in teams and the ability to compare one's individual performance with that of others are two of the most powerful motivators. The monitoring program described above is designed to take advantage of both of these motivational strategies.

5. The system provides teachers with useful feedback

on their performance. It has been said that teaching is the second most private act in which adults engage. Teachers generally work in a vacuum that separates them from other adults. The teacher who has no idea of how his or her students' perfomance compares to that of students in the next room, the next county, the state, or the nation is the norm rather than the exception. Peters and Waterman (1982) stressed that people cannot improve their performance when they work in a vacuum. Individuals need feedback and comparative information to help them assess and enhance their effectiveness. Schools must adopt feedback mechanisms in order to help teachers improve their performance.

When we discuss our ideas on monitoring with school administrators, we find that one of the most common concerns is that teachers will "teach to the test." Our response is a simple one: If the test reflects the important, designated outcomes of the course and effectively assesses student mastery of those outcomes, then the test is *exactly* what teachers should teach to! In other words, the test can help teachers and students focus on the most significant aspects of the course.

Occasionally we encounter administrators who enthusiastically embrace the idea of analyzing comparative teacher performance as a means of discovering "who the duds are." We gently try to emphasize that they have missed the point. The practice of providing comparative data to individuals is based on the following assumptions:

1. Most people believe they are good at what they do.
2. If teachers are given objective data demonstrating

that their performance is not as good as they thought it was, they will be motivated to find a way to reduce the discrepancy.

3. Such intrinsic motivation is generally more powerful than a negative evaluation from a supervisor.

If administrators introduce the idea of providing feedback on comparative performance as a means of identifying and weeding out poor teachers, many of the benefits of the program will be lost. Teachers are certain to rebel against a program based on a search and destroy mentality; such a program offers little to teachers. On the other hand, a positively orientated, comparative performance program encourages *all* teachers to consider how they might improve. Given the right climate, a teacher whose students scored above the school average on fourteen of the fifteen subtests of an examination will feel compelled to try to improve performance on that single deficient subtest. Given the right climate, teachers will turn to one another for ideas on improving performance. The right climate is one based on trust. We do not mean to suggest that administrators not seek to assist teachers whose students are consistently poor performers on examinations. We do recommend, however, that the program of providing teachers with comparative performance data not have as its primary focus the identification of weak teachers.

The results of testing can be reported in a variety of different ways—number of items answered correctly, average standard scores, frequency distributions, and so on. We agree with Lorin Anderson (1985, 1-2) that the format of reporting student scores that is most useful for decision making is "percent of students." Anderson explains how that format can be applied to different types of tests:

157

For teacher made tests, the percent of students achieving grades of A or B would be presented. For curriculum embedded tests, the percent of students mastering each objective would be presented. For state proficiency/competency tests, the percent of students who meet or exceed the overall standard would be presented. Finally, for nationally normed, commercially produced tests, the percent of students who fall in the highest and lowest national quartiles would be presented.

The percent of students format is useful in both establishing and monitoring school improvement plans. The faculty of Stevenson High School, for example, used the percent of students scoring at a particular level as the baseline data for each final examination, and then teachers set higher performance standards as part of their goal setting process. They found that the percent of students format provided an excellent means of referencing where the school was, where it wanted to be, and the progress it was making.

The percent of students format also simplifies the reporting and analysis of data. It is important to disaggregate achievement data in a number of ways in order to analyze the effect the instructional program has had on various groups of students. For example, many schools disaggregate their test data by reporting the scores of the students who qualify for free or reduced price lunches versus those of the students who do not qualify. Some districts also analyze their scores in terms of race or gender.

A point made in Chapter Five bears reemphasis here: Although testing should play a major role in any comprehensive program to monitor student achievement, traditional paper-and-pencil testing is clearly *not* the most appropriate method of assessment for *all* of the goals of a school. Much of what schools are trying to teach—the ability to write, to speak, to create, to demonstrate tolerance, to make responsible decisions—simply cannot be measured by a multiple-choice test. School leaders must work with teachers to identify and develop indicators of student achievement with respect to such goals.

MONITORING TEACHING

We believe that principals who truly value excellence in teaching demonstrate that belief by (1) implementing a supervision program designed to improve instruction and (2) devoting a significant amount of their time to observing teachers in the classroom.

Classroom Supervision: A Critique of the Traditional Model

Almost all models of teacher supervision and evaluation begin with the pronouncement that the primary purpose of classroom supervision is the improvement of instruction. Traditional programs of classroom supervision, however, have been more conducive to rating teacher performance than to bringing about any meaningful change in teaching.

In most schools a visit from the principal signals an inspection or a rating exercise rather that an effort to improve instruction. Using a checklist or rating scale, the principal may evaluate the teacher as "satisfactory" in classroom management, "excellent" in questioning techniques, "superior" in knowledge of subject matter, and so on. Whether the teacher is rated as superior or unsatisfactory generally has no bearing on his of her compensation, however, for in most school districts teachers are paid according to an established, lock-step salary schedule. Furthermore, once they have received tenure, they cannot be dismissed as a result of performance unless they are proven to be incompetent. Thus, for many teachers, the only effect of such a rating system is to determine whether or not their performance is minimally satisfactory. The system is, in effect, dichotomous, with "fail" represented by "unsatisfactory" and "pass" by all other rating levels. It is small wonder that teachers tend to regard such a system as either threatening or meaningless.

Many of those who defend the traditional approach to teacher supervision argue that periodic inspection helps keep the troops on their toes. However, as Naisbitt and Aburdene (1985) pointed out, outstanding companies have realized that unwilling employees cannot be supervised (in the traditional sense) into doing the job right. School administrators must come to the same realization. Those who believe that an annual observation and rating either motivates or helps teachers on a day-to-day basis are deluding themselves.

Another factor that has contributed to the sorry state of teacher supervision is lack of agreement as to what actually constitutes good teaching. Teachers frequently charge that they know more about teaching than the principal who is observing their class. Fortunately for educational leaders who are grappling with the problems of supervision, two recent developments have provided both a knowledge base for analyzing teaching practices and a process for supervising teaching. The knowledge base consists of the process-product research findings on effective teaching discussed in Chapter Five. The process for supervising teachers is the clinical supervision process.

Toward a Clinical Frame of Reference

The clinical approach to supervision was developed by Morris Cogan (1961, 3) and his colleagues through the Harvard-Newton program in the late 1960s. Some of the basic principles of clinical supervision are as follows:

1. The primary goal of clinical supervision is to improve instruction by observing, analyzing, and ultimately changing the behavior that takes place in the classroom.
2. Clinical supervision requires a face-to-face relationship between the supervisor and the teacher. As Robert Goldhammer (1969, 54) observed, "Clinical supervision is meant to imply supervision up close. . . . In every case the notion of face-to-face contact will be fundamental."
3. A major purpose of this approach to supervision is to help the teacher see, as objectively as possible, what is actually taking place in the classroom. Cogan emphasizes that the process is designed to deal with performance, not personality; behavior, not persons.
4. Clinical supervision works best when there is mutual trust between the supervisor and the teacher.
5. Clinical supervision encourages the professional and personal autonomy of the teacher.

A number of different writers have developed supervisory models based on the principles of clinical super-vision espoused by Cogan. We have found the model developed by Jerry Bellon (1982, 27-29) to be both practical and effective. It is currently being used in a number of school districts around the country. The Bellon model, which he refers to as synergetic supervi-sion, is based on the following six assumptions:

- People want to improve their performance.
- Objective feedback helps to improve performance.
- Pervasive patterns of teaching can be identified.
- When selected patterns of teaching are changed, instruction can be improved.
- Feedback to improve performance will be most effective when there is mutual trust.
- The primary goal of the supervision process is to improve instruction.

SYNERGETIC SUPERVISION

The synergetic supervision process consists of three stages: the pre-observation conference, the observation, and the post-observation conference.

The Pre-Observation Conference

The first step in the synergetic supervision process is a conference between the supervisor (generally the princi-pal) and the teacher. This brief (ten to fifteen-minute) conference takes place less that twenty-four hours before the observation. Its purpose is to provide the supervisor with an understanding of the teacher's plans prior to the actual observaton. The following points are discussed in the pre-observation conference.

1. *Learning context*

   - What is the relationship of the current unit of study to the course or program goals?

2. *Learner characteristics*

   - What are the students like? Are there students with special needs or characteristics?

3. *Learner objectives*

   a. Content objectives

   - What will students learn as a result of the lesson?

   b. Process objectives

   - What will the students be doing during the lesson?

4. *Assessment*

   a. Pre-assessment

   - What process was used to determine the level of student readiness for the lesson?

   b. Post-assessment

   - What process will be used to determine whether or not students have achieved the objective(s)?

5. *Instructional strategies and materials*

- What resources and teaching techniques will be utilized?

6. *Observer focus*

- What should be the major focus of the data collection effort by the supervisor?

The pre-observation conference is an important part of the supervision process for several reasons. First, it gives the supervisor an opportunity to learn the context of the particular lesson being observed—how it fits into the teacher's broader perspective on the curriculum and the class. The effectiveness of any teaching strategy must be addressed in relation to the objectives of a particular lesson planned for a particular group of students for a particular day.

Second, an effective pre-observation conference enables the supervisor to determine what types of data he or she should collect during the classroom observation in order to assess the effectiveness of the lesson.

Third, the conference provides the supervisor and the teacher with an opportunity to discuss the teacher's short and long-term instructional plans. This in itself, is helpful. As was pointed out in Chapter Six, planning is an important element of effective teaching. The pre-observation conference gives the supervisor a chance to assess the ability of the teacher in this critical area.

Fourth, the pre-observation conference is an excellent means of developing the trust that is a critical factor in effective supervision. Teachers generally appreciate the fact that the observer is making an attempt to understand their instructional plans. The supervisor should refrain from making value judgments or critiquing the teacher during this phase of the process; the conference should be viewed as a meeting of two professionals to discuss instructional goals and methods in a collegial manner. As Bellon concluded, (1982, 47) "If the pre-observation conference is properly conducted, the collegial relationship between teachers and administrators can be strengthened."

The Classroom Observation

The second phase of the synergetic supervision process, the classroom observation, allows the supervisor to watch the class and gather objective data relevant to the agreed upon focus. The supervisor is not a passive observer; during the observation he or she writes or charts what the teacher and students are saying and doing. Since it is the responsibility of the observer to collect accurate and useful data, he or she must strive to record what is actually happening in the classroom, not his or her feelings about what is happening.

The Post-Observation Conference

In the post-observation conference the supervisor and the teacher analyze and discuss the data during the classroom observation. The post observation conference encompasses four steps.

1. *Lesson* reconstruction. The supervisor and the teacher reconstruct what occurred in the classroom using the data collected and their recollections.
2. *Pattern identification.* The supervisor and the

teacher analyze the data to identify patterns or trends.

3. *Pattern assessment*. The supervisor and the teacher discuss whether each pattern was positive (helped to achieve the objective), negative (interfered with the achievement of the objective), or neutral.

4. *Planning for future instruction*. The supervisor and the teacher discuss the benefits of the positive patterns, identify strategies to eliminate negative patterns, and suggest areas of focus for the next observation.

Fischler (1971,174) likened this process to the theory of the discrepant event posited by Jean Piaget:

> The teacher, after looking at the record, analyzing what took place, searching for his patterns, categorizing his patterns as they relate to inhibiting or enhancing the objectives, and searching for alternate strategies that could be used to achieve the objective, is going through the process of assimilation, accommodation, and equilibration.

The entire cycle—pre-observation conference, observation, and post-observation conference—is repeated three or four times during the year in order to provide the teacher with feedback on the new instructional strategies being practiced. The effectiveness of the process depends on the ability of the supervisor in three areas:

1. *The ability to collect data during an observation*. A key factor in determining the quality of a post

166

observation conference is the richness of the data that have been collected. Did the observer have a focus that yielded high quality data? Was the observer able to collect sufficient data? Collecting data is a skill that can be developed only through practice.

2. *The ability to assess data.* A supervisor cannot help a teacher improve instruction unless the supervisor is a student of good teaching. Administrators cannot hope to become content specialists in all areas, but they can become process specialists. An impressive body of research on effective teaching has been developed in the past decade. Those responsible for teacher evaluation must first study that research and then help teachers to learn about it. Principals must serve as the link that unites the worlds of researchers and teachers.

3. *The ability to establish and maintain a trusting relationship with a teacher.* To paraphrase Bennis and Nanus (1985), trust is the oil that makes the supervisory processes work. Teachers will be unwilling to assess their teaching if they believe the principal will use that information in a punitive way. In order to develop the trust necessary for the process to be effective, an administrator must consistently demonstrate that he or she is trying to help the teacher improve instruction.

The Benefits of the Bellon Process

The synergetic sypervisory process offers several major advantages over the more traditional approaches of supervision.

1. *It enables teachers to analyze and improve their own*

instruction. A school could never hope to achieve excellence if the only time its teachers improved their effectiveness was when they were visited and rated by a supervisor. The synergetic process is designed to train teachers to analyze, adjust, and improve their instruction on an ongoing basis. The post-observation feedback they receive about their teaching enables them to become more conscious of their teaching patterns. Furthermore, the discussion of the effectiveness of patterns is a form of individual staff development that helps the teacher become more aware of the research on effective teaching. Positive teaching strategies are reinforced, and teachers are alerted to tendencies or strategies that may be ineffective. Teachers are then able to use the skills and information that they have acquired through this process to monitor and assess their effectiveness even when the principal is not observing.

2. *It alerts the principal to areas in need of staff development.* The process enables the principal to identify the needs of individual teachers for additional training and staff development, as well as the general needs of the staff as a whole.

3. *It enhances the concept of the principal as both leader and empowerer of teachers.* As mentioned earlier, a major emphasis of this program is to eliminate the need for teachers to rely on others to assess their effectiveness. As teachers are empowered to assess the impact of their teaching, they become the kind of professionals that Naisbett and Aburdene (1985) claimed will be needed for organizations of the future—people willing to assume responsibility, take initiative, and monitor their own work. The principal, in turn, becomes a kind of transforma-

tional leader who helps develop and nurture those with whom he or she works. Thus the synergetic process is designed to enable the principal to act as both a strong leader and an empowerer of teachers. As Bellon (1971,4) wrote:

The clinical process can be a helpful process for the instructional leader in his effort to improve classroom instruction. However, the ultimate goal should be to help the teacher develop an analytical approach about his own classroom behavior.

STRATEGIES FOR MONITORING STUDENT ACHIEVEMENT AND CLASSROOM INSTRUCTION

Monitoring is such a key element in developing excellent schools that it cannot be left to chance. School leaders must monitor all components of the improvement program of a school, but the areas of student achievement and instructional effectiveness merit special attention. Following are some strategies we recommend to school leaders interested in monitoring student achievement and classroom instruction:

1. Review your procedures for monitoring student achievement in light of the recommendations offered by the *Effective Schools Report* (1983). Do you provide locally developed tests that are curriculum based, criterion referenced, and nationally normed?

How closely do the standardized tests you utilize match the curriculum of the school?

2. Ask teachers to develop common measures of assessing student achievement. At the high school level this should include common, comprehensive final examinations that are administered at the end of each course. Grade school teachers should develop and administer common unit tests following key units of instruction.

3. Review what is done with the data collected as a result of efforts to monitor student achievement. Is the information provided by the testing program used in curriculum decision making? Are teachers able to apply the test results to instructional decision making?

4. Provide each teacher with information regarding the test performance of his or her students compared to that of similar students in the school, in the district, in the state, and in the nation.

5. Accumulate student test performance data over time so that you can provide teachers with a historical comparison of the performance of their students. Contact Sam Ritchie (Adlai E. Stevenson High School, 16070 W. Highway 22, Prairie View, Il 60069) for information on a computer program that can provide teachers with comparative achievement data.

6. Assess your current instructional supervision progam. Is its focus clearly on improvement rather than on rating?

7. Read *Classroom Supervision* and *Instructional Improvement: A Synergetic Process* by Jerry and Elnor Bellon (1982) for a more detailed explanation of the

instructional supervision program described in this chapter.

8. Discuss possible changes in the staff supervision program with the faculty. You may want to try a new supervisory program with a small group of teachers before undertaking a full scale implementation.

CHAPTER EIGHT

Celebrating
The Success of
Your School

In the absence of ceremony or ritual, important values have
no impact.

Terry Deal and Allen Kennedy (1982,63) *Corporate Cultures*

A number of different studies have concluded that the
public receives most of its information regarding schools
from students, the media, and the schools themselves.
For a number of reasons, this news should be of major
concern to anyone interested in creating an excellent
school.

When the baby boomers were moving through the
public schools in the 1960s, over half of the adults in the
United States had children in school. Today only about
one-fourth of the adult population has school-aged children. Thus fewer people receive information about
schools and education on a daily basis. Conversely, more
people than ever before rely on the media for information
regarding public education. This fact gives educators
little reason to rejoice. The national media have tended
to paint a bleak picture of public education. The attention given by the media to the emotion-laden rhetoric of
the *Nation at Risk* report, to the exclusion of other
educational reports that were better researched and

more balanced, is only the most recent indication of this tendency.

But far worse than the image of schools presented by the media is that generated by schools themselves. Schools are their own worst enemy in terms of adversely affecting public opinion. A few years ago contestants on the popular television quiz show, "Family Feud" were asked to respond to the following question: "You have just received a call from your child's school. Why has the school called?" The same question had been asked to a hundred members of the show's studio audience. The five responses selected most frequently were:

- He has misbehaved.
- He is failing.
- He is doing poor work/missing assignments.
- He is ill/injured.
- He is truant.

This sampling suggests that the most neutral statement parents could hope to hear from a school was that their child was sick. Educators bombard parents with negative messages and then are puzzled when parents react negatively to the schools.

The tendency of educators to stress problems or failures when communicating with the public stands in marked contrast to the practices of the nation's most successful businesses. In their study of America's best-run companies, Peters and Waterman (1982) observed that excellent companies create systems specifically designed not only to produce lots of winners, but also to celebrate winning once it occurs. To satisfy people's desire to be a part of a winning team, these companies continually seek to provide evidence of the success of the organization. And to satisfy the human need to stand out and be recognized for individual ability, they celebrate the efforts and achievements of individuals within the organization. In their analysis of effective business practices, Deal and Kenndy (1982, 60) were emphatic about the importance of celebration to the success of a business organization; they concluded that "a corporate culture, and the values it embodies, must be ritualized and celebrated if it is going to survive."

Schools should heed these messages. There is no evidence to suggest that educators are immune from what Ernst Becker (1973) described as humanity's "essential dualism"—the need to feel both a part of a significant collective endeavor and a star in one's own right. Nor is there evidence to suggest that these yearnings affect only adults. Those interested in spurring a school to excellence should make a systematic and sustained effort to celebrate the success of its teachers and students, both within the school and the larger community.

WORKING WITH THE STAFF

In any organzation a sense of excellence must start from within. Students, parents, and members of the larger community will never develop a high regard for a school unless the staff members within it have that high regard first. Dr. Jerry Bellon (1984), who has consulted in school districts throughout the United States, observed that although he has seen some communities overestimate the quality of their schools and others that don't fully appreciate the job their schools are doing, he has never seen a community which holds its schools in higher regard than the faculty does.

Thus the question becomes "What can be done to instill a sense of pride among those who work in the school." Chapters One and Two discussed the importance of drafting a statement of mission and communicating values. However, once the mission and guiding values have been identified, it is equally important to reinforce them at every opportunity. Celebrating the evidence of these values is the most effective means of providing such reinforcement. Those interested in promoting excellence in a school should consider the following recommendations.

Provide Evidence of The School's Success

School leaders must recognize people's innate desire to be on a winning team, and continually seek to provide evidence of their success. There is much in education that is quantifiable—achievement test scores, passing rates, attendance rates, levels of student participation in co-curricular activities, and so on. A concerted effort to monitor, report, and extol the gains that occur in such areas will promote a sense of excellence. Those who dismiss improvements in such areas as insignificant are making a major mistake. The celebrations that surrond the delivery record of Frito-Lay employees or the sales achievements of Mary Kay Cosmetics representatives do not just fete the delivery of corn chips or the sale of makeup. These corporate celebrations promote specific cultural values, establish norms for others to emulate, and convey a sense of the effectiveness of the organization and its people.

Effective companies use celebrations to promote the attitude "we will succeed because we are special." As that attitude becomes engrained in an organization, it is ultimately recognized by those outside of the organization as well. Deal and Kennedy (1982) illustrated this point with the example of the sales representative who says, "I'm with IBM" rather than "I peddle typewriters for a living." Because of the outstanding reputation that IBM enjoys, the simple statement "I'm with IBM," serves as a source of personal satisfaction for the sales representative. Furthermore, it heightens his or her expectations for personal performance. Deal and Kennedy concluded that the attitude "we will succeed because we are special" can be maintained only by continually celebrating achievements that reflect the values of the organization. Thus those interested in promoting particular values within a school must always be on the lookout for indicators of the presence of those values. Teachers must be given evidence that their efforts are having an impact.

Establish a reward structure to ensure lots of winners

There is a tendency on the part of those interested in creating excellent schools to establish exceptionally high standards in order to demonstrate the school's commitment to excellence. (Generally those high standards are set by one group for achievement by another—administrators for teachers, teachers for students, and so on.) Peters and Waterman (1982) found this same tendency at work in most companies. However, they also found that the effect of this policy was to ensure that the majority of people in the organization failed to achieve the targets and thus failed to benefit from the company reward system. Employees began to think of themselves as losers and, in time, began acting as losers.

Peters and Waterman found that just the reverse was true of the excellent companies they studied. These companies created reward systems designed to guarantee that most of the people would meet their goals, which were often set by the employees themselves. Thus these companies reinforced the perception of their employees that they were doing well, a perception that psychologists have found to be one of the prime factors in motivation. By providing their employees with an opportunity to be winners, excellent companies capitalize on the fact that we all want to think of ourselves as winners.

There are undoubtedly those who would dismiss this example from the business world as irrelevant to education because of the reliance of schools on public funding. "We would love to offer more rewards for our teachers," they would argue, "but we cannot use public funds for bonuses when we can't afford new textbooks." Such an assertion is understandable, but it misses the point. Peters and Waterman found that excellent companies make extraordinary use of nonmonetary incentives. In fact, these companies tend toward small, symbolic rewards rather than large, lucrative ones. Peters and Waterman (1982, 58) offered the following caution:

> Big bonuses often become political, and they discourage legions of wokers who don't get them but think they deserve them. . . . The small reward, the symbolic one, becomes a cause for positive celebration rather than the focus of a negative political battle.

Deal and Kennedy (1982) cited a company that has captured the essence of the small symbolic reward with its "Attaboy" award. The award itself is a simple inexpensive plaque, but it is presented with great fanfare. A manager rings a bell, and all work comes to a halt as everyone gathers around. With great flourish the manager presents the award, announcing something to the effect of "By the power vested in me, I hereby present this award of one great big "Attaboy" to _____ in return for his (her) exemplary service." There is enough humor in the award to make it more fun than competitive. "Employees can't take the ceremony seriously, but it is a very serious ceremony," concluded Deal and Kennedy (1982, 61). "Managers earning $150,000 a year or more earnestly compete for these plaques."

Schools are fertile ground for programs involving the awarding of small symbolic rewards to staff members in recognition of a job well done. Schools would do well to scrap such honors as the "Teacher of the Year" award, which creates one winner and an entire faculty of losers, and replace them with programs that recognize and reward all those who help advance the school toward its vision.

Make a conscious effort to make heroes of staff members

According to Deal and Kennedy, effective managers extol the virtues of exemplary employees day in and day out at the slightest sign of successful behavior. If a school is to be excellent, its administrators must recognize that one of their most important responsibilities is to identify and publicize the efforts and achievements of staff members that reflect the values of the school. There are at least three reasons why this responsibility should be given priority:

1. *Recognition improves the morale of those singled out.* Public recognition of exceptional effort is certain to have a positive motivational effect on the recipient of that recognition. In treating someone as a star, we increase the likelihood that the individual will in fact act like a star.
2. *Recognition affects others on the staff.* People tend to assess their own performance not according to some arbitrary standard, but in relationship to the performance of others. As Deal and Kennedy (1982,38) concluded,

> People can't aspire to be "good" or "successful" or "smart" or "productive", no matter how much management encourages them in those directions. They can, however, aspire to be like someone: "He's just an ordinary person but look how successful he is. I can be successful like that too."

By recognizing the performance of individual staff members, administrators provide the remaining staff members with a model and motivate them to engage in similar behavior.

3. *Public recognition reinforces the values of the school.* Recognition serves as a reminder of what is important.

Here are some specific suggestions school officials might use to make heroes of their staffs.

- Invite parents to write letters of commendation for teachers who have gone above and beyond the call of duty or who have been extremely effective. With the permission of parents and teachers, periodically publish excerpts from these letters in a newsletter to the staff.

- Establish a program similar to the "Attaboy" award described previously.

- Devote one section of the school's parent newsletter to a regular feature highlighting faculty accomplishments.

- Send frequent personal letters of commendation and thanks, and place copies of these letters in the teachers' personnel folders. Remember Lee Iacocca's (1984) advice to admonish face to face but praise in writing.

- Publicize the achievement of faculty members through every conceivable means—press releases, newsletters, sign boards, daily announcements, special bulletins, resolutions from the board of education, public award ceremonies, and so on.

- Encourage teachers to share their expertise by making presentations at professional meetings or contributing to professional journals. One district sets aside a special fund to cover the travel expenses of any teacher selected to make a presentation at a state, regional, or national conference. Not only is such exposure good for the school, but it is a tremendous means of providing a teacher with a sense of recognition. Administrators in the district should actively support their teachers' proposals for presentations by writing letters of recommendation or endorsement to the professional organization.

- Watch for opportunities to nominate deserving teachers for awards sponsored by external organizations.

Two points bear re-emphasis. First, in order to be effective, an award program must provide for a wide distribution of awards. A school with only a handful of outstanding teachers will have a difficult time achieving excellence. The reward system should make *all* teachers feel that they have an opportunity to be recognized as outstanding. Second, an achievement need not be monumental to warrant celebration. It is impotant to vigilaently seek out the small successes—those teachers whose students performed well on a competitive exam or in a co-curricular contest, who attracted exceptional student enrollment, who modeled their academic discipline by practicing it outside of the classroom, who earned advanced degrees, who contributed to their professional organizations, or who were acknowledged as having made a difference in a student's life. These teachers merit the recognition of the school community.

Schedule Periodic Opportunities for the Staff to Come Together in a Social Setting

Effective organizations use frequent informal gatherings and organizational ceremonies to promote a spirit of oneness and to showcase star performers. These gatherings can be as informal as the Friday afternoon "beer bust" attended by the employees of the Tandem Company or as formal as a black tie awards dinner. Successful organizations also recognize that ceremonies held to welcome new members into the organization or honor members retiring from the organization provide excellent opportunities to promote the values of the organization.

Here are just a few ways in which school leaders can make use of social gatherings to celebrate success.

- *Provide extensive, ongoing orientation programs for new staff members.* The typical orientation program for new teachers consists of a single day devoted to the explanation of bureaucratic procedures. An orientation program should have the inculcation of the school's values as its primary objective. The program should continue throughout the year, with administrators getting together with new staff members every other week or so to answer their questions and reinforce key values. Furthermore, school leaders who are really interested in promoting a vision of the school will not restrict their orientation efforts to teachers but will also orient secretaries, clerks, custodians, and all of the other employees of the school.

- *Develop annual rituals that bring staff members together.* One outstanding school sponsors a series of rituals over the course of the school year. The school year begins with a board-staff dinner for all employees and their spouses. Co-curricular sponsors are feted later each fall at a beer and bratwurst picnic. Throughout the year the staff enters teams in the school's intramural athletic program. In December staff members bring their children to school when Santa Claus comes to visit. Faculty teams compete in a schoolwide trivia contest one evening in January. From February through April, all staff members are invited to join a weight reduction/fitness program which culminates in a party financed by the fines of those who could not meet their weight-loss goals. In May the principal hosts a cocktail party in honor of the teachers given tenure. The year comes to an end with a staff appreciation brunch, at which staff members with perfect attendance and those who have reached a milestone in their seniority (five years, ten years, etc.) are presented awards. These frequent opportunities to get together have created a sense of unity among the staff. Although teacheres are not required to come to the school's graduation ceremony, which is held on a Sunday afternoon after the school year has ended, they feel such loyalty to the school and to its students that nearly 90 percent of them attend.

- *Use retirements as an opportunity to demonstrate appreciation for staff.* Effective leaders recognize the adverse effect that an uncelebrated retirement can have on an organization. When someone who has devoted years to an organization is allowed to leave it with little ado, those who remain look upon the organization's lack of appreciation as a sign that their efforts will go unrecognized as well. The school described above turns the retirement of each staff member into a roast complete with amusing speeches, shared memories, and gag gifts. The roast provides an excellent blend of humor and sentiment, but most important it makes a star out of someone who has contributed to the school.

FULFILLING THE PROMISE OF EDUCATION

WORKING WITH STUDENTS

The reasons given above for recognizing and celebrating the achievements of staff members apply to students as well. Students too will benefit from the perception that they attend a high quality school and that they are achieving success and recognition in it. Many of the studies of the effects of positive reinforcement and praise have taken place in the educational setting. Thus it is ironic that educators generally have failed to take advantage of the power of positive reinforcement. The following sugggestions are offered as examples of ways schools can celebrate the success of students.

Send Parents Positive Reports on the Performance of Their Children

The response of the "Family Feud" audience referred to at the beginning of this chapter provides an indication of how infrequently schools send parents positive messages about the performance of their children. One elementary school addressed this problem by printing a picture of the school on postcards and encouraging teachers to use these cards to let parents know when their students are showing improvement or are doing well. In that community, a picture of the school has thus become associated with good news about children.

A positive approach to progress reports is more difficult to implement in a high school setting, where the student load of individual teachers may run as high as 150 or more. However, software programs are available that enable teachers to send a computer-generated letter simply by circling the name of a student and a number that corresponds to a particular message such as

184

"Just wanted you to know that _____ has been making excellent contributions to class discussion." An administration that makes such a program available to teachers provides a means of getting positive messages to parents and at the same time demonstrates an awareness of teachers' time.

Expand The Practice of Awarding School Letters

If the practice of awarding school letters is designed to both motivate students and build their pride in the school, it seems obvious that schools in search of excellence should seek to expand the opportunities to present such letters. One high school awards letters to all those who participate in athletics rather than limiting the award to those who score a certain number of points or play a minimum number of games. The same school also awards letters to students involved in co-curricular activities such as drama, choir, band, debate, the math team, and the school newspaper. Finally, the school presents letters to students who make the high honor roll for the entire year. Walking the halls of this school, one notes that almost all the students are wearing letter jackets, and one can sense the pride these students take in their school.

Increase the Recognition Given to Students Who Achieve the Honor Roll

Too often, the only action taken by schools to recognize the students who achieve the honor roll is to issue a press release to the local newspapers. One school that is determined to celebrate the achievements of its students maintains a large scroll on which are listed the names of all students who made the honor roll in the previous grading period. The scroll is displayed prominently in the main entry area of the school. At the end of each grading period, honor roll students are invited to a continental breakfast with the faculty. Faculty members take full advantage of this opportunity to commend and reinforce the achievement of these students. The principal sends a congratulatory letter to the parents of each honor roll student, and area businesses provide free passes to movies, free hamburgers, and other rewards to those students. At the end of the year, the superintendent hosts a banquet for students who have achieved the high honor roll throughout the year. These efforts have made it clear to the entire school community that this school honors academic performance.

Establish a "Student-of-the-Week" Program

A student-of-the-week program honors students for exceptional service or achievement. A picture of the student is placed on display, along with narrative describing his or her achievement. Daily announcements call attention to the award. Anyone in the school can nominate a student for this honor.

Turn Your Honors/Awards Ceremony into an Extravaganza

One high school in the suburban Chicago area presents and annual awards ceremony that rivals a Hollywood production. The ceremony is entirely planned and produced by students. Elaborate sets complete with waterfalls, fountains, and curved staircases transform the auditorium stage. A script is written for the entire production. The students who act as masters of ceremony are dressed in tuxedoes and long dresses. The school orchestra provides musical interludes as students come forward to accept their awards. Television cameras pan the audience, zooming in on winners as their names are announced. Large-screen televisions placed throughout the auditorium show their reactions to the audience. School officials make no effort to hide the fact that the ceremony is based heavily on the Academy Awards Show. After all, the very purpose of their awards program is to make students feel like stars.

Use Graduation Ceremonies to Honor Student Achievement

Schools often make the mistake of using their graduation ceremonies to focus attention on a valedictorian and a salutatorian to the exclusion of all other students. Such a system is effective in recognizing the students ranked first and second in the graduating class; however, the student ranked third is not even acknowledged. Many schools are now moving to the practice, common in colleges, of having honor-level graduates rather than a valedictorian and salutatorian. Different categories of honors are established, such as highest honors, high honors, and honors. Students in the various categories are then given a distinguishing accoutrement for their caps and gowns, such as a sash, cord, or pin, and are featured in the graduation program. Thus, instead of honoring two graduates, the graduation ceremony can honor the achievements of a significant number of the class members.

Advise Students of the Success of Their School and Their Peers

A school interested in promoting particular values should utilize every means to publicize the presence of those values, including announcements, press releases, newsletters, special bulletins, signs, display cases, and public ceremonies. Officials should continually advise the school community (particularly the students) of individual and collective achievements that reflect the values of the school.

STRATEGIES FOR CELEBRATING SUCCESS

One important way to further the quest for excellence is to give those within a school a sense that the school is succeeding and that their individual contributions to its success are recognized and appreciated. By celebrating efforts and achievements that reflect the values of the school, school officials can reinforce the behavior of those who are recognized, provide models for others in the organization, and emphasize what is considered important in that school. The standards for achievement should not be set so high as to make recognition infrequent or exclusive; they should be designed to make stars of as many people as possible. Following are some strategies we recommend to school officials interested in celebrating success:

1. Provide evidence of the school's success to those within it. Look for improvements, trends, or accomplishments that can be reported in a positive light.
2. Establish a reward structure that ensures lots of

winners. Remember that small symbolic awards are more effective than large ones, which tend to become political.

3. Make heroes of staff members through such means as publishing excerpts from letters of commendation, featuring faculty accomplishments in school newsletters and other available media, sending frequent letters of congratulations and appreciation, providing support (both emotional and financial) to enable teachers to contribute to their professional organizations, and nominating deserving teachers for awards sponsored by external organizations.

4. Use frequent informal gatherings and official ceremonies to promote a spirit of oneness and to showcase star performers.

5. Initiate a program to provide parents with positive reports on the performance of their students.

6. Expand the criteria for awarding school letters to include participation in co-curricular activities as well as academic achievement.

7. Increase the recognition given to students who achieve the honor roll by posting their names in the school, sending them and their parents congratulatory letters, hosting a brunch or dinner in their honor, and persuading area businesses to provide them with rewards.

8. Establish a "student-of-the-week" program to honor students for outstanding service or achievement.

9. Turn your honors/awards program into an extravaganza.

10. Increase the number of students recognized at graduation by establishing different categories of honor graduates.

CHAPTER NINE:

Persistence: Sustaining The Improvement Process

> Nothing in the world can take the place of persistence. Talent will not; nothing is more common than unsuccessful men with great talent. Genius will not; unrewarded genius is almost a proverb. Education will not; the world is full of educated derelicts. Persistence, determination alone are omnipotent.

Calvin Coolidge (1926)

Implied in the concept of school improvement is the gradual process of change—change both within individuals and organizations as a whole. This process must be sustained over an extended period of time if genuine improvement is to take place. Many school improvement programs start with a flourish but lose momentum in the third, fourth, and fifth years. Remembering how often they have been called upon to embrace a new program only to see the interest of the district wane and the program sputter and die, teachers are likely to respond to yet another improvement program with the ho-hum attitude of "this too shall pass." This attitude is almost certain to be one of the major obstacles on the path to excellence.

BARRIERS TO CHANGE IN SCHOOLS

Writers have offered a number of different theories as to why schools are so slow to accept change. Richard Carlson (1965) suggested that because they do not confront the competitive pressure to change that businesses face, schools have slowly become "domesticated." Like domesticated animals, schools have become accustomed to a guaranteed existence and thus have lost the incentive to change which arises out of the struggle for survival.

Another barrier to change cited by Carlson (1965, 5) is a weak knowledge base: "It is rare indeed when an educational innovation is backed by solid research. It is even rarer to find an educational innovation which has been fully developed and subjected to careful trial and experimentation." Whereas in agriculture a prototypical farm is often established to persuade farmers of the benefits of new methods and materials, schools are largely left to their own devices when contemplating or initiating change.

Neale, Bailey, and Ross (1981) added two more barriers to those described by Carlson. First, they pointed out that change in education is hampered by the fact that Americans disagree about the goals of education. Second, they suggested that schools are resistant to change simply because they are human organizations and all human organisms seek a state of equilibrium.

Change suggests at least temporary disequilibrium and thus is viewed as something to be avoided.

ORGANIZATIONAL HEALTH: A KEY TO SUCCESSFUL CHANGE

Despite the obstacles, some schools do succeed in initiating and sustaining change. How do they do it? Matthew Miles (1965 p.13) argued that it is the health of the organization rather than the content, the quality, or the demonstrated efficacy of a particular educational innovation that determines whether or not it will be adopted and used effectively. "Organizational health," Miles contended, "can tell us more than anything about the probable success of any change."

What makes for a "healthy" organization? Miles listed ten interconnected dimensions that reflect organizational health. Although a simple listing of the dimensions does not do justice to the complexity of the concept, it does provide a starting point for analyzing the health of a particular organization. The ten dimensions are as follows:

1. *Goal focus.* A healthy organization has clearly defined, achievable goals that most members of the organization accept.
2. *Communication adequacy.* The adequate flow of information within the organization is a basic characteristic of a healthy organization.
3. *Optimal power equalization.* A healthy organization distributes power in a relatively equitable manner. Subordinates can influence bosses and perceive that bosses can do likewise.

192

4. *Resource utilization.* A healthy organization makes effective use of the inputs (resources) of the system, particularly human resources.
5. *Cohesiveness.* A healthy organization has a common identity. The members are attracted to and can relate to the organization and its purposes.
6. *Morale.* In a healthy organization, people feel good about working. Organizational morale implies feelings of well-being, satisfaction, and pleasure.
7. *Innovativeness.* A healthy organization tends to be more innovative than an unhealthy organization over a period of time. It will grow, develop, and change rather than continue with routine, standard procedures.
8. *Autonomy.* Members of a healthy organization believe that they are responsible for their own destiny. They do not view themselves as being tools of the larger outside environment.
9. *Adaptation.* A healthy organization adapts in realistic, effective ways to the environment. Autonomy does not imply immunity from outside influences.
10. *Problem-solving adequacy.* All organizations have problems. A healthy organization is not one that is free of problems, but rather one that has a way of dealing with problems as they arise.

A recent study of innovative companies by Rosabeth Moss Kanter produced similar findings. Kanter (1983, 32-33) found that innovative companies were characterized by "integrative thinking," which encouraged the treatment of problems as a whole:

> Such organizations reduce rancorous conflict and isolation between organizational units;

create mechanisms for exchange of information and new ideas across organizational boundaries; ensure that multiple perspectives will be taken into account in decisions; and provide coherence and direction to the whole organization . . . . Work is done in an environment of mutual respect, participating teams, multiple ties, and relationships that crisscross the organization chart. Furthermore, the large amount of on-the-job socializing that takes place around innovating organizations is not merely an "enlightened fringe benefit"; it serves an important task-related purpose: building a foundation of cross-cutting relationships to make integrative team formation that much easier.

In contrast to the integrative thinking of the innovative companies, Kanter (1983, 33) found a "segmentalist approach" among companies resistant to change:

Segmentalist approaches see problems as narrowly as possible, independently of their context, independent of their connections to any other problems. Companies with segmentalist cultures are likely to have segmented structures: a large number of compartments walled off from one another—department from department, level above from level below, field office from headquarters, labor from management, or men from women.

Unfortunately, Kanter's description of the segmentalist culture aptly depicts many school districts. All too frequently schools are characterized by rigid departmental structures, adversarial relationships between teachers and administrators and territorial disputes among staff members. Purkey and Smith (1983) described schools as loosely-coupled systems in which classrooms are isolated workplaces subject to little organizational control. One elementary school principal was less generous, describing his faculty as "twenty-four different people in twenty-four different rooms united by a common parking lot." Schools must escape from this segmentalist thinking if they are ever to become receptive to significant change.

THE PROCESS OF CHANGE: IMPLICATIONS FOR STAFF DEVELOPMENT

Even within a healthy organization, the process of change takes place in increments over an extended period of time. One of the most frequently cited models of the process of change is that of Everett Rogers (1962). In his book, *Diffusion of Innovations*, Rogers divided the process into five stages: (1) awareness, (2) interest, (3) evaluation, (4) trial, and (5) adoption. Although he described these stages in relation to the individual, they can easily be applied to organizations.

1. *Awareness.* At this stage the individual has been exposed to the new idea or knowledge but is not yet motivated to seek further information. The importance of the awareness stage lies in the fact that it is a logical prerequisite for the later stages.

195

2. *Interest.* In the interest stage the individual becomes interested in or perhaps curious about the innovation or idea and seeks additional information about it. No judgment is reached as to the usefulness of the innovation at this stage.
3. *Evaluation.* In the evaluation stage the individual mentally applies the innovation to a present or future situation and then decides whether or not to try it. Rogers described this stage as a "mental trial." It is at this stage that the individual develops and opinion about the innovation. Whereas the previous stage is cognitively oriented, in the evaluation stage the emphasis is on the affective domain.
4. *Trial.* In the trial stage the individual conducts a dry run, utilizing the idea or information on a small scale in order to decide whether or not it is useful in his or her situation. Rogers believes that most people will not adopt an innovation without first trying it out.
5. *Adoption.* In the adoption stage the individual considers the trial results. If they are favorable, the idea or innovation is utilized to an even greater degree.

This model of the change process suggests that no matter how thoroughly the usefulness of an idea has been confirmed through statistical validation by researchers or even trial validation by funding authorities, most teachers need to try it in their own classrooms before they will embrace it fully. Bob Eaker and Jim Huffman (1980) developed a consumer-validation approach to staff development that recognizes this aspect of the change process. Their approach is based on the assumption that before teachers will be willing to become "consumers" of research, they must first act as "testers" to determine the effects of implementing the findings in their classroom. The consumer-validation procedure includes three steps:

1. *Research reporting seminars.* The primary purpose of these seminars is to provide teachers with a clear understanding of research findings on a particular topic such as time on task, questioning strategies, or classroom management. The findings are synthesized and presented as clearly and concisely as possible. Teachers are then invited to brainstorm specific activities or strategies for implementing the research findings in their classrooms.
2. *Classroom implementation.* During the next three to four weeks, teachers apply the research by initiating some of the strategies or activities that were identified in the brainstorming sessions. In short, teachers are asked to reflect upon and evaluate the results of their efforts. Forms are provided on which the teachers can briefly describe the activities and strategies they attempted and their reactions to what occurred.
3. *Sharing sessions.* In this final stage the seminar groups reconvene and teachers share their findings. These sessions serve two important purposes. First, the pooling of information gives teachers new ideas to try in their own classrooms. The "testimonial" of a colleague is of tremendous value in motivating teachers to pursue an idea. Teachers tend to hold the experiences of a colleague in much higher regard than the findings of a researcher. Second, the sessions give teachers and opportunity to interact with each other about teaching. Unfortunately, teaching is rarely the subject of meetings that teachers are asked to attend. Simply increasing the dialogue

among teachers on the topic of teaching can have a positive effect on a faculty's sense of professionalism. The recognition that teachers need an opportunity to try out proposals for change is also a key feature of a model of staff development offered by Bruce Joyce and Beverly Showers (1983). They proposed that the following elements be included in training programs for staff members.

1. *Recognition of the difficulty of transfer.* It is difficult to transfer new information or new skills into everyday practice. Even though a new skill has been explained and demonstrated, staff members are likely to need practice and coaching before they are actually able to include the skill in their repertoire.
2. *A high degree of skill development.* It is simply not reasonable to expect that poorly developed skills will be transferred. Thorough training conducted over an adequate amount of time is essential for effective staff development.
3. *Development of executive control.* Teachers must have the intellectual "scaffolding" necessary not only to perform a skill, but also to judge when its use is appropriate. As Joyce and Showers (1983, 22) noted, "Not until a teacher can select the strategy when it is appropriate to do so, modifying it to fit the characteristics of the student, implement it, and assess its effectiveness can we say he or she has achieved an adequate degree of executive control".
4. *Practice in the workplace.* Practice is a necessary ingredient for skill development. When more learning is needed, more practice is required.
5. *Coaching.* Teachers often need assistance from someone who has mastered the skills that they are

trying to learn. Joyce and Showers advocate coaching as part of staff development for the following reasons:

a. *The provision of companionship.* By providing for interaction with another human being, coaching gives teachers the support they need to tackle a difficult process.
b. *The provision for technical feedback.* Coaching provides teachers with feedback as they practice new models of teaching.
c. *The analysis of application.* Coaching helps teachers analyze what they might accomplish by making further adjustments.
d. *Adaptation to students.* Coaching helps teachers "read" the responses of their students. Teachers need to be able to read responses correctly in order to decide whether they need further training in how they might adapt the particular skill they are practicing.

6. *Promotion of the ability to "learn how to learn."* The ultimate goal of staff development should be to help teachers develop the ability to add to their teaching skills at will. Thus Joyce and Showers stressed the importance of programs that help teachers develop a learning aptitude which empowers them to learn in new situations and to solve problems as they arise.

Whatever model a school district chooses to follow in its staff development program, it is important that the program demonstrate the commitment of the district to the continuing development of its people. Excellent businesses recognize that the nurturing and development of their human resources must be a priority if the organization is to prosper. In 1984 IBM spent nearly $700 million on training and development. The contrast between IBM's commitment to the development of human resources and that of most school districts is a clear indication of the inadequacy of the latter.

THE IMPORTANCE OF PERSISTENCE

Those who set out on the quest for school excellence must do so with the clear understanding that they can never permit themselves to feel that they have arrived at their destination. As Peters and Austin (1985) observed, the bad news about the pursuit of excellence is that you'll never finish. Toynbee's (1958, 50) description of civilization applies also to the pursuit of excellence: "it is a movement . . . and not a condition, a journey and not a destination, a voyage and not a harbor." An organization cannot be static; it is in either a state of growth or a state of decay. As efforts to improve in some areas of a school run their course, efforts to improve in other areas must be initiated. John Gardner (1963, 5) described the process of self-renewal this way:

> Our thinking about growth and decay is dominated by the image of a single life-span, animal or vegetable. Seedling, full flower and death. "The flower that once has blown forever dies." But for an ever-renewing society the appropriate image is a total garden, a balanced aquarium or other ecological system. Some things are being born, other things are

flourishing, still other things are dying, but the system lives on.

How can a leader sustain the effort to change when the goal is so elusive and timeless? The answer, the *only* answer, is persistence. As Admiral Hyman Rickover (19, 415) observed, "Good ideas and innovations must be driven into existence by courageous patience." Naisbitt and Aburdene (1985) contended that people are energized by the vision of an organization only when it is not only powerful but persistent. When Bennis and Nanus (1985, 187-99) asked ninety leaders about personal qualities they needed to run their organizations, they found that "they never mentioned charisma, or dressing for success, or time management, or any of the other glib formulas that pass for wisdom in the popular press. Instead, they talked about persistence and self-knowledge; about willingness to take risks and accept losses; about commitment, consistency and challenge".

Theodore Friend III (1985), past president of Swarthmore College observed:

> "Leadership is heading into the wind with such knowledge of oneself and such collaborative energy as to move others to wish to follow. The angle into the wind is less important than choosing one and sticking reasonably to it."

We hope that this book has offered valuable assistance to local school leaders in choosing their angle into the wind. The most significant factor in determining one's eventual destination, however, is the ability and courage with which one stays the course. The future of the excellence movement in education lies not in national reports or state legislatures, but in the effort of those committed to improving their local schools. We wish them Godspeed.

STRATEGIES FOR SUSTAINING CHANGE

1. Be persistent.
2. Be persistent.
3. Be persistent.
4. Be persistent.
5. Be persistent.

BIBLIOGRAPHY

Adler, Mortimer, J. 1982. *The Paideia Proposal: An Educational Manifesto*. New York: Macmillan.

Anderson, Lorin. 1985. "Frequent Monitoring of Student Progress." Paper presented at South Carolina Conference on Public Schools, Charleston, South Carolina.

Armistead, Law. 1982. *Building Confidence in Education*. Reston, Va.: National Association of Secondary School Principals.

Becker, Ernst. 1973. *Denial of Death*. New York: Free Press.

Bellon, Jerry. 1971. "Clinical Supervision." Unpublished paper, University of Tennessee.

Bellon, Jerry, 1984. "The Teacher as Instructional Leader." Speech presented at Lake County Teachers Instituts, Gurnee, Illinois.

Bellon, Jerry, and Bellon, Elnor. 1982. *Classroom Supervision and Instructional Improvement: A Synergetic Process* 2nd ed. Dubuque, Iowa: Kendall-Hunt Publishing.

Benniis, Warren, and Nanus, Burt. 1985. *Leaders: The Strategies for Taking Charge*. New York: Harper and Row.

Berman, Paul, and McLaughlin, Milbrey W. 1975. *Federal Programs Supporting Education and Change,*

Vol. IV: The Findings in Review. Santa Monica, Calif.: Rand Corporation.

Blanchard, Kenneth, and Johnson, Spencer. 1983. *The One-Minute Manager.* New York: Berkley Books.

Blumberg, A., and Greenfield, W. 1980. *The Effective Principal.* Boston: Allyn and Bacon.

Boyer, Ernest. 1983. *High School: A Report on Secondary Education in America.* New York: Harper and Row.

Boyer, Ernest. 1985. "In the Aftermath of Excellence." *Educational Leadership*, March, pp. 10-13.

Brookover, Wilbur, and Lezotte, Lawrence. 1979. *Changes in School Characteristics Coincident with Changes in Student Achievement.* East Lansing: Michigan State University, Institute for Research on Teaching.

Brookover, Wilbur; Beamer, Laurence; Efthim, Helen; Hathaway, Douglas; Lezotte, Lawrence; Miller, Stephen; Passalacqua, Joseph; and Tornatzky, Louis. 1982. *Creating Effective Schools.* Holmes Beach, Fla.: Learning Publications.

Brophy, Jere. 1979. "Teacher Behavior and Its Effects." Occasional Paper 25, Institute for Research on Teaching, Michigan State University, East Lansing:

Brophy, Jere, and Good, Thomas L. 1986. *In Handbook on Research on Teaching,* 3rd ed.; edited by Merlin C. Whittrock. New York: Macmillan.

Burns, James McGregor. 1978. *Leadership.* New York: Harper and Row.

California State Department of Education. 1977. *School Effectiveness Study: The First Year.* Sacramento, Calif.: California Department of Education, Office of Program Evaluation and Research.

Carlson, Richard O. 1965. "Barriers to Change in Public Schools." In *Change Processes in the Public Schools.* Eugene, Ore.: Center for the Advanced Study of Educational Administration.

Carnegie Foundation Forum on Education and the Economy. 1986. *A Nation Prepared: Teachers for the 21st Century.* Washington, D.C.: Carnegie Foundation.

Casteen, John. 1985. "The Influence of Leadership, Power, and Authority." In *In Honor of Excellence.* Reston, Va.: National Association of Secondary School Principals.

Cawelti, Gordon. 1984. "Behavior Patterns of Effective Principals." *Educational Leadership*, February, p. 3.

Cogan, Morris, L. 1961. *Supervision at the Harvard-Newton Summer School.* Cambridge, Mass.: Harvard University.

Coolidge, Calvin. 1926. In *Leaders: Strategies for Taking Charge*, by Warren Bennis and Burt Nanus. New York: Harper and Row, 1985.

Deal, Terrence, and Kennedy, Allan, 1982. *Corporate*

Cultures: The Rites and Rituals of Corporate Life. Reading, Mass.: Addison-Wesley.

Discipline in the Public Schools. 1984. Arlington, Va.: Educational Research Service, April.

D'Israeli, Issac. 1834. "Curiosities of Literature." In *Bartlett's Familiar Quotations*, 15th ed. Boston: Little, Brown, 1980.

Dreikurs, Rudolf, and Grey, Loren. 1968. *Logical Consequences: A New Approach to Discipline.* New York: Hawthorn.

Eaker, Robert, and Huffman, James. 1980. Occasional Paper 44, Institute for Research on Teaching, Michigan State University, East Lansing.

Edmonds, Ron. 1979. "Effective Schools for the Urban Poor." *Educational Leadership*, October, pp. 15-23.

Edmonds, Ron. 1982. "On School Improvement: A Conversation with Ron Edmonds." *Educational Leadership*, December, pp. 12-15.

Effective Principal: A Research Summary. 1982. Reston, Va.: National Association of Secondary School Principals.

Effective School Report. 1983. Jackson, Miss.: November.

Effective Schools: A Summary of Research. 1983. Arlington, Va.: Educational Research Service.

Eisner, Jane. 1979. "Good Schools Have Quality Principals." In *The Journalism Research Fellows Report: What Makes and Effective School*, edited by D. Brundage. Washington, D.C.: Institute for Educational Leadership, George Washington University.

Finn, Chester, 1985. "The Dilemmas of Educational Excellence." In *Honor of Excellence*. Reston, Va.: National Association of Secondary School Principals.

Fischler, Abraham. 1971. "Confrontation: Changing Teacher Behavior Through Clinical Supervision." In *Improving In-Service Education: Proposals and Procedures for Change*, edited by Louis J. Rubin. Boston: Allyn and Bacon.

"The Five Correlates of an Effective School." 1983. In *Effective School Report*. Jackson, Miss.: November, p. 4.

Friend, Theodore. 1985. In *Leaders: The Strategies for Taking Charge*, by Warren Bennis and Burt Nanus. New York: Harper and Row.

Gardner, John. 1961. *Excellence: Can We Be Equal and Excellent Too?* New York: Harper and Row.

Gardner, John 1963. *Self-Renewal: The Individual and the Innovative Society*. New York: Harper and Row.

Garfield, Charles. 1986. *Peak Performers: The New Heroes of American Business*. New York: William Morris.

Goldhammer, Keith, and Becker, George. 1972. *Elementary School Principals and Their Schools*. Eugene,

Ore.: Center for the Advanced Study of Educational Administration.

Goldhammer, Robert. 1969. *Clinical Supervision.* New York: Holt, Rinehart and Winston.

Goodlad, John. 1985. In *Pride and Promise: Schools of Excellence for All the People,* by Mary Anne Raywid, Charles Tesconi, and Donald Warren. Westbury, N.Y.: American Educational Studies Association.

Goodlad, John. 1984. *A Place Called School: Prospects for the Future.* New York: McGraw-Hill.

Herzberg, Frederick. 1966. *Work and the Nature of Man.* New York: World.

Iacocca, Lee, and Novak, William. 1984. *Iacocca: An Autobiography.* New York: Bantam Books.

In Honor of Excellence. 1985. Reston, Va.: National Association of Secondary School Principals.

Joyce, Bruce, and Showers, Beverly. 1983. *Power in Staff Development Through Research on Training.* Alexandria, Va.: Association of Supervision and Curriculum Development.

Kanter, Rosabeth Moss. 1983. *The Change Masters: Innovation and Entrepreneurship in the American Corporation.* New York: Simon And Schuster.

Kelley, Edgar A. 1980. *Improving School Climate.* Reston, Va.: National Association of Secondary School Principals.

Kroc, Ray. 1970. In *Leaders: Stragegies for Taking Charge*, by Warren Bennis and Burt Nanus. New York: Harper and Row, 1985.

Lewis, James, Jr. 1986. *Achieving Excellence in Our Schools . . . by Taking Lessons from America's Best-Run Companies*. Westbury, N.Y: Wilkerson Publishing.

Lewis Karen Seashore. 1986. "Reforming Secondary Schools: A Critique and Agenda for Administrators." *Educational Leadership,* September, pp. 33-36.

Lipham, James. 1982. *Effective Principal, Effective School*. Reston, Va.: National Association of Secondary School Principals.

Miles, Matthew B. 1965. "Planned Change and Organizational Health." In *Change Processes in the Public Schools*. Eugene, Ore.: Center for the Advanced Study of Educational Adminsitration.

Naisbitt, John, and Aburdene, Patricia. 1985. *Reinventing the Corporation*. New York: Warner Books.

National Commission on Education. 1983. *A Nation at Risk: The Imperative for Educational Reform*. Washington, D.C.: U.S. Government Printing Office.

Neale, Daniel C.; Bailey, William J.; and Ross, Billy E. 1981. *Strategies for School Improvement*. Boston: Allyn and Bacon.

New York State Department of Education. 1974. *Reading Achievement Related to Educational and Environ-*

mental Conditions in 12 New York City Elementary Schools. Albany: Division of Educational Evaluation.

Norris, B. 1986. "Bennet Foresees A Business Model." *Times* Educational Supplement, August 29, p. 11.

Onward to Excellence: Making Schools More Effective. 1984. Portland, Ore.: Northwest Regional Educational Laboratory.

Peters, Thomas, and Austin, Nancy. 1985. *A Passion for Excellence: The Leadership Difference.* New York: Random House.

Peters, Thomas, and Waterman, Robert, Jr. 1982. *In Search of Excellence: Lessons from America's Best-Run Companies.* New York: Harper and Row.

Phi Delta Kappa. 1980. *Why Do Some Urban Schools Succeed?* Bloomington, Ind.: Phi Delta Kappa.

Presidential Task Force on School Violence and Discipline. 1984. In *Discipline in the Public Schools.* Arlington, Va.: Educational Research Service, April.

Process Evaluation: A Comprehensive Study of Outliers. 1978. Baltimore: Center of Educational Research and Development, University of Maryland, February.

Purkey, Stewart, and Smith, Marshall. 1983. "Effective Schools: A Review.: *Elementary School Journal,* March, pp. 427-452.

Raywid, Mary Anne; Tesconi, Charles; and Warren, Donald. 1985. *Prides and Promise: Schools of Excel-*

lence for All the People. Westbury, N.Y.: American Educational Studies Association.

Rickover, Hyman, 1985. In *A Passion for Excellence,* by Thomas Peters and Nancy Austin. New York: Random House.

Rogers, Everett. 1962. *Diffusion of Innovations.* New York: Macmillan.

Rutter, Michael; Maughan, Barbara; Mortimore, Peter; Ouston, Janet; and Smith, Alan. 1979. *Fifteen Thousand Hours.* Cambridge, Mass.: Harvard University Press.

Selznick, Phillip. 1957. *Leadership in Administration: A Sociological Interpretation.* New York: Harper and Row.

Sergiovani, Thomas. 1967. "Factors Which Affect Satisfaction and Dissatisfaction of Teachers." *Journal of Educational Administration,* pp. 66-82.

Shaw, George Bernard. 1973. *Man and Superman.* Baltimore; Penguin Books.

Sizer, Theodore. 1984. *A Review and Comment on the National Reports on Education.* Reston, Va.: National Association of Secondary School Principals.

Sizer, Theodore. 1985. "The Student-Teacher Triad." In *In Honor of Excellence.* Reston, Va.: National Association of Secondary School Principals.

Taba, Hilda. 1962. *Curriculum Development: Theory and Practice.* New York: Harcourt, Brace and World.

"Teachers Want More Control of the Work Place . . . but only One-Fourth Are Empowered." 1986. *Education U.S.A.*, April 21, p. 4.

Thompson, Scot. 1980. In *Improving School Climate*, by Edgar A. Kelley. Reston, Va.: National Association of Secondary School Principals.

Toynbee, Arnold. 1958. "The Graeco-Roman Civilization." *Civilizations on Trial*. London: World Publishing.

U.S. Department of Education. 1986. *What Works: Research about Teaching and Learning*. Washington, D.C.: U.S. Department of Education.

United States Senate Resolution 359. 1979. In *Effective Principal, Effective School*, by James Lipham. Reston, Va.: National Association of Secondary School Principals, 1981.

Ventures in Good Schooling: A Cooperative Model for Successful Secondary School. 1986. Reston, Va.: National Association of Secondary School Principals.

Waterman, Robert. 1985. In *A Passion for Excellence*. Thomas Peters and Nancy Austin. New York: Random House.

Weber, George. 1971. *"Inner City School Children Can Be Taught to Read: Four Successful Schools."* Occassional Paper 18, Council for Basic Education, Washington, D.C.

INDEX

INDEX